Change Your Life

Mussar with the Messiah

Vickie Howard

AuthorHouse™
1663 Liberty Drive
Bloomington, IN 47403
www.authorhouse.com
Phone: 1-800-839-8640

© 2010 Vickie Howard. All rights reserved.

No part of this book may be reproduced, stored in a retrieval system, or transmitted by any means without the written permission of the author.

First published by AuthorHouse 7/23/2010

ISBN: 978-1-4490-4670-5 (sc)
ISBN: 978-1-4490-4671-2 (hc)

Printed in the United States of America
Bloomington, Indiana

This book is printed on acid-free paper.
Library of Congress Control Number: 2009911833

All Scripture references from: The Scriptures Bible Institute for Scripture Research/USA, Follow The Pattern Ministries, unless otherwise quoted.

All quotes from Pirkei Avos reproduced from Ethics of the Fathers, by Rabbi Moshe Liber with permission of the copyright holders, Art Scroll/Mesorah Publications. Ltd. It may not be further reproduced or copied without specific written permission.

All quotes from Rabbi Rami Shapiro: excerpts are from The Sacred Art of Lovingkindness Preparing to Practice ©2009 by Rami Shapiro. Permission granted by Skylight Paths Publishing, Woodstock VT www.skylightpaths.com

All quotes from Rabbi Ralph Messer of Simchat Torah Beit Midrash, Denver Colorado, permission granted. Quotes and teachings may not be further reproduced or copied without specific written permission from STBM, www.Torah.tv

All quotes from Alan Morinis: excerpts are either from Climbing Jacob's Ladder or Everyday Holiness, The Path of Mussar, permission granted from Alan Morinis. Quotes may not be further reproduced or copied without specific written permission from Mr. Morinis www.mussarinstitute.org

Dedicated to my loving husband, Jay and my fantastic children, Max, Hannah, Sophie, Sam and Ray. Thank you for your patience as I typed away. And to my gracious Mom, thank you for your support and belief in me. Thank you YHWH!
Thank you T. Logan for proofing.

Introduction

My husband and I have been born again for quite a while. Our children live in a home in which we pray together, pray for one another and pray for others. We try and glorify God in all we do and keep Him as the substance of our lives. We believe and have taught our children that Yeshua has paid the price of redemption that we are a set apart people and ought to behave as such.

We are also human and we can bicker, complain and whine like the best of them. We stumble and fall, ask for forgiveness and go on. We stress in our house to be quick to forgive and quick to ask forgiveness.

In 2006 I was diagnosed with stage IIIB breast cancer. I had a double mastectomy, 19 lymph nodes removed, 6 rounds of chemotherapy and 7 weeks of daily radiation.

My husband Jay was there every step of the way for me, and I was and am continually grateful to him. He was increasingly patient with me as I cried after the surgery, and cried as I tried to take showers with the 'drains' hanging from me. He even removed the last two drains that were protruding from my chest wall, all before leading a Sabbath study.

There were mornings that I just did not want to wake up. There were those 'chemo' days that I didn't want to go, I was so done. But Jay kept encouraging me, telling me just 5 more treatments, just 4 more, and three more and so on. He drove me every day to get the radiation treatments, and bought me two gorgeous wigs.

We promised each other to never bicker or argue again, as we knew how very precious life was and how short it truly can be.

Guess what, the bickering, even though we had sincere intentions, continued.

I just couldn't believe that a husband and a wife who had just gone through what we had survived would pick up again with our fleshly old ways. But we did.

Then The Father revealed something so very important to me. It was my character trait, my emotions that could run out of control that were spurring on the feelings of offense, the pride and the arguing. It was me and it was him. It was us.

My daughter randomly bought a book about Mussar for Jay as a gift. It was random in my mindset, but God always has a bigger plan. I borrowed the book and devoured it. I knew then that it wasn't by chance that God had brought that book into my life. As I read through it, I saw Yeshua through and through, even though in traditional Mussar He is never mentioned. The chapters sparked so many Scripture Verses that reminded me of Yeshua. He is the Perfect One and we are perfected through Him. He was/is Mussar!

But why weren't we behaving as such? Why were some people so calm and I could flare up so easily? Mussar taught me the basics that I should have known. I needed to change. I needed to work with God in changing me to glorify Him.

Yes, I am a new creature in the Messiah, but my DNA is still my DNA and my emotions are still my emotions and my character traits are still my character traits.

The Mussar teachings revealed so much. It is our work, plus our discipline through Yeshua that will change us. Unclean behavior is something that we acquire and learn. Unclean behavior can be in our soul traits, lurking, waiting to pounce. Inappropriate behavior can be encouraged at an early age by the environment or parents, but this behavior can be stopped and changed.

I love Yeshua and I want to be the best I can be. I hope that this book will help you too. I want to encourage you so don't give up. You are a perfect creation of God. You are His child. You are a wonderful, flawlessly made person. There are no mistakes that come from God. There are no 'woops, I didn't see that coming..' from God. We create the inaccuracy. We create the issue. Whether it is coming from our forefathers or our own emotions, the blunders are ours to take credit for.

I am not a doctor, nor do I hold a PHD in anything. I am a home schooling mom of 5, a devoted rancher and Pastors' wife. I make many mistakes, oh so many. I don't claim to have all the answers, but I have peace in Yeshua/Jesus and am ever striving to better myself. That is the purpose of this book. To share what has helped me. Just as if you had a severe cold, I would share my special 1,000mg of vitamin C drink.

I had the opportunity to practice every one of these traits in the days preparing for The Pesach, Passover. The enemy was hard at work towards our family, our lives and our congregation.

We put on a public Seder every year. It is a beautiful night, full of praise music, wonderful dances, anointed teachings, to which over one hundred attend. Of course, hasatan does not want any of this to take place, and he is there lurking about to tempt us in our faults so that we may lose our temper, become agitated, or worse yet, quit the whole thing.

Needless to say, I was able to practice the very essence of what I had learned and what I wanted to bring to others. And I am continuing in the journey!

In fact, I continued to continue this journey of being an imperfect soul during the printing of this book. Upon sending in the final manuscript, it was published. The publisher then sent me a hard and soft copy of the book. I was thrilled! I flipped through the pages and found not one but two errors! Panic gripped me. I stopped the printing, and explained to the publisher that there were errors and that I needed everything shut down; I would be sending them a different manuscript. A very good friend offered to proof the book and she found many errors. Even to the point that the numbers of Scripture verses were displaced. (Dyslexia?) How awful to misrepresent Scripture verses!

But then to my horror, I discovered that a few books, the not so good copies, were sold. How humiliating! So many character traits raced through my very essence of my soul!

YHWH is forever molding us, shaping us, dealing with us and through us. My pride was wounded. I was embarrassed to have anyone with a bad copy. And then God so graciously gave me the answer: Fix it. Apologize to those that bought a bad copy, and send them a better copy. I am solely responsible for any and all of my errors and any and all glory goes to The Father. Always.

So, this book is a book for life. A book of life. I don't know if we ever out grow our temperaments. It is possible that we get them in check, in order, and under control – with the help from the Divine Source, The Father.

In the English language 'peace' is a noun. But in the Scriptures it is a verb. Peace is a tangible thing. So, I would like to give you peace as you mark the beginning of a new you.

Y'varekh'kha Adonai v'yishmerekha
Ya'er Adonai panav eleikha vichunekka.
Yissa Adonai panav elekha v'yasem l'kha shalom.
May The Lord bless you and keep you
May The Lord make His face shine on you and show you favor
May The Lord lift up His face toward you and give you peace.

Blessings to you.

Shalom!

Vickie Howard

PS. If anyone has a crummy copy, I'll send you a good one. Thank you for your forgiveness.

"Wake up my brothers! A guest you've never seen has arrived! Once he leaves you will never see him again."

"Who is this guest?" They asked.

Said R' Dov Ber: "Today!"

In this book, I use the titles *YHWH*, Lord, God, Yeshua, Jesus, *Adonai, Elohim* interchangeable.

I was saved in 1989 by crying out to 'Jesus'. I later learned that His Hebrew name is Yeshua, also learning about the name *YHWH*. The reason why I decided to use different titles is that each one of us is at a different place. Pastor Jay Howard of Simchat HaMashiach Beit Emunah, Durango Colorado, teaches that The Name is more than just a name: it is a walk, a lifestyle. How true!

I can parade around all day saying *Yod Hey Vav Hey* and Yeshua, yet gossip about my neighbor and cheat on my spouse. Neither is it how well I pronounce it. It is The Walk. How I am walking, what I am doing, how am I behaving? What are my actions?

I also quote different Rabbis' and their teachings. Some are old, some new. But make no mistake; the greatest Rabbi that ever walked was Yeshua. He is the Prince of Peace, the King of Kings, Lord of Hosts and Lord of The Living. He is The Living God and The Redeemer. I love Him and owe my everything to Him.

Contents

Part 1	Peace For Your Soul	1
	The Path	3
	Understanding Emotions	9
	Mapping It All Out	15
	What is Mussar	21
	The Purpose of Living	29
	Our Generational Curses	37
	The Battle Within	45
	The Dream	51
	Putting it into Practice	57
	Review	67
	The Character Traits	71
Part 2	Letting Go and Changing Mussar in Practice	77
	Beginning	79
	Equanimity	87
	Patience	99
	Joy	111
	Order	121
	Truth	131
	Silence	145
	Humility	157
	Loving-kindness	167

Part 3	Finishing The Character Traits And Choosing Life	177
	The Phases of Mussar	179
	Gratitude	187
	Compassion	195
	Generosity	203
	Enthusiasm	211
	Honor	219
	Trust	229
	Faith	239
	Forgiveness	249
	Keep Moving Forward	261

PEACE FOR YOUR SOUL

PART ONE

> In Israel, in order to be a realist you must believe in miracles."
>
> -David Ben-Gurion, Oct. 5, 1956

The Path

In the study of Mussar, there are a number of character traits that are explored, adjusted and worked on. In one course there were thirteen, in another 15, and yet another 28. Of course one could add or delete, depending on their nature, and their personal traits. One of the reasons for thirteen is because we are taught there are thirteen attributes of God, and these thirteen attributes of compassion of God, are recited on *Yom Kippur.*

One trait that was listed was *Yirah*, a Hebrew word that is not easily translated into English. Its meaning is rich and intertwined. Two English words, fear and awe compound the word *Yirah*. How can a word mean both fear and awe?

When I think of seeing The Messiah return in His Glory, I can't imagine the splendor of it. It is beyond human understanding and comprehension. But, in this earthly state, I can imagine that I would feel fear of the glory, brightness and loudness, and at the same time be in such awe of the glory, brightness and loudness of His Triumphant return.

King Solomon, who made silver in Jerusalem as common as stones; I Kings *1Melakim* 10:27; and who desired the wisdom of God, wrote, *"Let us hear the conclusion of the entire matter: Fear God and guard His commands, for this is the whole of man."* Ecclesiastics *Qoheleth* 12:13

"I know that whatever God does is forever. There is no adding to it, and there is no taking from it. God does it that men should fear before Him." Ecclesiastes *Qoheleth* 3:14

Think of a sunset and the delicate beauty of a rainbow. All the glory of the colors, the hues, the absolute perfect arrangement of the oranges and pinks, and vivid purples. Could we make a sunset? Could we make a rainbow? Think of the human body and how our blood pumps endlessly through a muscle, the heart. Think of our eyes that see His Glory, our ears to hear the sounds He gives us and our fingers that transfer the touch signals to our brains. Consider about our minds, our thoughts that invent such magnificent things.

"*Lord our Lord how magnificent is Your Name through out the earth.*" Psalms, *Tehillim* 8:9

This bestows fear and awe at the same time. Knowing that God put the beat in my heart, and I as a human do not know the day or time or season when it will stop beating, gives me fear and awe of The Holy One, The King of Kings, at the same time.

Alan Morinis in his book, *Climbing Jacobs Ladder* quotes Rabbi Perr as saying that "there is such a thing as ethics without the fear of God." But, that does not mean we should associate God with the fear of punishment. God is our deliverer, our Savior, our shield, our healer, our life. That is fear and awe in the same breath.

"*The fear (awe) of God is a fountain of life, to turn away from the snares of death.*" Proverbs *Mishle'* 14:27

"*The fear (awe) of God is the beginning of knowledge.*" Proverbs *Mishle'* 1:7

"*He has sent redemption to His people; He has commanded His covenant forever. Set apart and awesome is His Name. The fear of God is the beginning of wisdom...*" Psalms *Tehillim* 111:9, 10.

Notice that Psalms 111:9, 10 has fear and awesome in the same context. It is His name, His walk, His ways, His Son. So it is with this understanding that He made you. You are a child of The Most High with a divine purpose and a divine plan.

Bill Pagaran of Broken Walls stood in front of the students at the Native Cultural Center at Fort Lewis College, Durango Colorado and explained this: He took a twenty dollar bill and asked which student wanted it. Of course all of them raised their hands. He then crumpled it up and asked the same question. He got the same response; all of the students raised their hand. He then spit on the bill, tore off an edge, stomped on it and crumpled it up some more. Again, he asked the question of the students, who wanted the twenty dollar bill? And again, all the students raised their hands. He then told the students that they were like that twenty dollar bill. As the twenty is worth its value, so were they. Even when crumpled or spit upon, it still had the value of a twenty dollar bill. He gave that twenty dollar bill to a young student with tears in her eyes. As Bill told the students, "You are not an 'oops'." [1]

Whatever your age, whatever your story, you were created as a perfect human being in The Eyes of God.

You are The Glory of God. He created you in His image, in His likeness. We tend to think of a physical form, but God is Spirit, and we worship Him in Truth and Spirit. And what is God? God is the Torah, The Living Word. It is already in you, it is already created within you. God's presence is within you and you are His perfect creation.

Our Traits

Some traits must be exhibited often, some traits very little with great caution and care. It can be compared to preparing a meal. Too much salt will ruin the challa, but no salt and it will be lacking in flavor.

Some such traits that should be adopted in large measures are loving kindness, patience and humility. Other traits that should be used sparingly and with caution are fear, anger and harshness. Some character traits that would be better off redefined are arrogance and unforgiveness.

"And just as pain, distress and afflictions indicate bodily illness, so evil traits indicate sickness of the soul. And just as to men are physically ill bitter tastes sweet and sweet bitter and there are those sick men who desire food that is not good for them and hate food that is good for them…' The Ways of The Tzaddikim.[2]

I stood in one section, in one corner, of the religious part of a bookstore in Phoenix Arizona. I was amazed at all the books written to Christians for their well being. To get a better life. To live a better life. To have a better life. To leave a pit. To get out of a hole. To find one's purpose. Books and books and books on self help to walk as we are supposed to walk in order to be a happier and more joyful me. Is this the panacea of life, to be happy?

I was confused on which one would best suit an individual. I wondered, is life so awful? Is life so sad? I think that most everyone would want to be better, happier, and more joyful. Don't we all think we have to search for our purpose in live? Don't we all at sometimes try to 'find' our purpose, our being in life? Wouldn't a common goal of most of us be to have the best marriage they can, the best children they can raise and to be a loving person?

I can read and read on how I should behave, but if I don't know what to correct, it will be like putting a band aid on a broken leg. How frustrating to know how I should behave, but can't get there! It's like seeing the other side of the river and the bridge is out. Well, we're going to rebuild that bridge. Even if it has to be one block at a time.

Remember God's will is not what we may perceive it should be. *"For My thoughts are not your thoughts, neither are your ways My ways," declares The Lord.* Isaiah, *Yeshayahu* 55:8

His will is written in the Scriptures, His will for me is to walk in His commands and praise His Holy name, to take care of His people, to be loving and kind. To be a Holy People. *"Speak to all the congregation of the children of Israel and say to them, 'Be set-apart, for I YHWH your Elohim am set-apart."* Leviticus, *Wayyiqra* 19:2

God moves us in and out of seasons and people. Our purpose is His ultimate purpose and His brilliance is seen in His ability to work the various parts and players together into a large story that serves His ultimate purpose.

So, in order to be that happier and more joyful 'us', let's correct some character traits for the sake of Him, not for the sake of ourselves. Let's glorify Him in our demeanor, our actions, and our ways. Life is not about us but about Him.

A story:

Mr. and Mrs. S live in an area where they heat with wood. During the day when Mr. S was at work, Mrs. S brought in wood trying to help, not realizing it was the wrong size of wood for that particular stove. Upon arrival home, Mr. S told her that the wood was wrong and now he would have to go out (it was late and winter dark) and get wood himself. Mrs. S became very agitated and stormed out of the house and began to pack in wood. Mr. S followed her out to the wood stack and loudly began to tell her to get away, it was his job. An argument began, and voices escalated. She barged ahead, he pushed her back, and then she slapped him. She lost her temper and then he lost his, and began yelling at her. Finally, exhausted, they went to bed in separate sleeping areas.

The next morning, after zero sleep, both Mr. and Mrs. S met in the kitchen where the coffee was on, each one feeling quite foolish. Both said they were sorry and the normal busy weekday began. Life did not stand still for either one of them. The sun still rose, and the clock still ticked on.

But, they did lose some of *their* precious time that The Father had allowed them. They lost those precious moments of peace with each other and sleep. For a brief space in time, they *lost* each other.

Mr. and Mrs. S have been married almost 25 years. They have children. They believe in God and His Son. They are mature educated people. They love each other dearly. How does something so ridiculous happen to good willed people?

Examine the character and soul traits that may have ignited this ordeal.

Here is a possible list:

Selfishness: poor me now I have to bring in wood
Offense: I brought in wood, he should say thanks
Anger: I'll show him, I'll just bring in more wood
Pride: how dare she, that's my job, I'll bring in wood
Pride: don't tell me what to do
Pride: oh yes I will
Very short temper/anger: Slap (she to him)
Anger: Yelling constantly
Pride: both to bed alone and he/she should apologize

It happens quite easily to good willed people. It happens to loving couples and to parents towards their children. It does happen, and can happen, but it doesn't have to. It can be corrected. In a natural sense, people do not want to behave poorly, the discontentment you may feel is the catalyst for your change.[3]

As it is written in *The Ways of The Tzaddikim*, "*Therefore, all men must be informed that anyone who wishes to attain worthy character traits must intermix fear (awe) of Hashem with each trait, for fear (awe) of Hashem is the common bond among all traits. This may be compared to a string which has been strung through the holes of pearls, with a knot tied at its end to hold the pearls. There is no question that if the knot is cut all the pearls will fall.*"[4] Parenthesis mine.

1. Broken Walls, Bill Paragan www.brokenwalls.com
2. The Ways of the Tzaddikim Feldheim Publishers
3. Rabbi Ralph Messer, Simchat Torah Beit Midrash Denver CO
4. The Ways of the Tzaddikim Feldheim Publishers

The hardest part of a job is getting started

Understanding Emotions

Character traits and soul traits define a person. They are what we are. Character traits are manifested in verbal and non verbal ways. They are feelings, emotions, and gestures. Many aspects of your personality affect the way others view you.

The basics are:

- Ability to follow through
- Beliefs
- Communication style
- Devotion
- Fairness
- Honesty
- Initiative
- Sincerity
- Truthfulness
- Values

It is our responsibility to decide how we want to be truthfully perceived by others. We can put up a façade, a front that tells others what we think we are, or what we would like to be, but that will dissipate in time. So, we really need to look at ourselves. No holding back. Remember the old cartoon? 'I have met the enemy and it is I'.

Communication plays a huge factor in our daily lives. How am I communicating to that person? Is that person connecting with what I am trying to convey? What is that person really communicating to me? Do I understand all the signals?

There are communication factors and there are also walls that can stop effective communication. [1]

Communication model factors can be but are not limited to:

The *environment* in which you send and receive messages will affect how you communicate.

The *sender* becomes your role if you send the message.

The *receiver* will be you until you respond to the message.

The *message* is the idea you are conveying.

The *channel* is how you send your message, in person, telephone, letter, etc.

The *encoding* occurs as you evaluate how to send your message, what language, and gestures.

Decoding occurs when you convert the message you receive back into ideas and interpret the meaning.

The *feedback* is a crucial element of the two way communication process.

Filters are factors that can distort or affect the message that is received. They can include your interests, attitude, issues, and belief as well as others.

Noise actually can mean the volume level of the message, or the clarity that can interfere with any accurate reception of a message.

There are also barriers to communication. Some of those can be:

- Preconceived ideas (my belief system)
- Emotions
- Evaluation of sender (I can disqualifying them in my mind)
- Distractions
- Word usage
- Being inconsistent with non-verbal & verbal communication
- Distrust

Albert Mehrabian, did a great study on communication. It was found that 38 percent of message meaning comes from vocal qualities such as speech rate, pitch, volume and articulation rather than from just the spoken word. And the nonverbal cues, our face and body language make up another 55 percent. Mehrabian found that when the non-verbal gestures and behavior contradicts the verbal spoken message, the meaning of the message and the spoken words becomes altered and other messages are conveyed. [2]

There are preferred and non preferred verbal usages in our language that will convey what we really mean. For instance, when you say "The problem is…" are you really focusing on only negatives? Aren't you really pointing the finger and blame at some one? It would be better to say, "The issue is…"

Another ideal sentence would be "I apologize for…" rather than saying, "I need (want) you to…"[3] That way you are putting the problem in your court. "I apologize for not making myself clear"…or… "I apologize for misreading you." Doesn't that happen all too often?

Many of us use verbal highlighters to get our meaning across or to get feedback. These can be positive or negative highlighters. When someone is conveying a message to a coworker and constantly repeating 'Right? Right?' they are in actuality wanting an agreement with the receiver of the message. Whether it is a control issue or a lack of self confidence, they are pushing for a 'yes' mode from the receiver of his message. Whether the receiver agrees or not isn't the issue, the sender is pushing for that 'right', that affirmation, or approval.

The role of non-verbal communication is just as important if not more important than our verbal communication. For instance, if a person is nodding and complying with someone who is the sender of a message, yet their arms are folded tightly across their chest, or they are sitting in a chair with their legs crossed and one leg is moving quickly, what are they really conveying to the sender of the person? At any given moment in time your whole body posture reflects your emotional state.

Pastor Jay Howard of Simchat haMashiach Beit Emunah included in one of his lessons, walking upright, *yesharun* with YHWH. If we are in a state of unworthiness, what will our posture be? Standing upright or slumped over? If we are living with and because and in YHWH and not in self debasement or arrogance, we will have a *yesharun* (upright) posture. We will be confident because and in and through The Lord. So, what do our verbal cues tell others?

We also need to be careful how we may view non-verbal communication and not let our emotions and opinions enter in to judging that person.

Some typical non-verbal cues may match, and most likely will match our emotion and our character traits.

- Posture. By standing up straight and walking upright one conveys a message different than by walking slumped over or walking hunched over (not from physical ailments).
- Eye Contact. There are so many different messages that can be sent to the sender or receiver of a message by the act of looking at a person in the eyes, or by staring. Also, the non-verbal gesture of not looking the person in the eye takes on a totally different concept. Are they lying?
- Nodding. Usually means agreement.

- Smiling. Usually is always viewed as a warm and friendly gesture. It may also be used as a front for embarrassment or uneasiness.
- Crossing the arms across the chest usually means a closed and defiant gesture. (it could also signal being cold).
- Pointing a finger or an object at a person. This gesture is usually viewed as being rude and challenging.
- Hands on hips. This is almost always viewed as defiant and authoritarian.
- Hand gestures and touch. These can send a multitude of messages, either positive or negative. Grabbing a person's elbow can exhibit a control issue, where a soft pat on the back can convey encouragement.

Non-verbal cue interpretation is important in looking at ourselves and others. It is important to identify the behavior such as; why are we tapping the pencil? Why are we clicking the pen? Or "I've noticed you've been fidgeting as we talk..."[4]

It is important that we ask for meaning and clarification in ourselves and others. For example: What am I thinking and what do my signals that I am conveying mean? And, "Please tell me what you are thinking... is there an issue?"

Giving feed back is equally important, too. It allows the other person the grace in knowing that we may have perceived their non-verbal communication wrongly and unjustly. "Did I say something wrong?" rather than, "Why are you doing that?"

Conflict

No one likes conflict in their lives. My mother is constantly saying that she is too old for discourse. That may be true, but it is through the conflict, if it is used in a positive and healthy manner, that we see where the discourse is coming from.

Conflict results in our behavioral issues, our character traits and issues of the heart. It is usually derived from one person being annoyed with the others personality, opinions, or ideas.

To deal effectively with conflict we must learn to recognize its sources:

- Differing values and beliefs: Are the values and beliefs interfering with understanding of the person's life and opinions.

- Varying perceptions: Are the issues in my life keeping me from the true perception of the other person.
- Inadequate or poor communication: Am I really communicating properly to the other person, or am I expecting them to know what I am thinking or trying to communicate.
- Goals that don't match: Have we expressed or explained our goals properly and thoroughly to the other person.
- Personal style differences: Am I taking into account the other person's upbringing, lifestyle, religion, etc.
- Contrary Expectations: Am I expecting one thing out of a situation and the other party is expecting another.

All these factors tie in with our emotional habits, our character traits and soul traits. All of these factors may and can tie into the issues of the heart.

1. Effective Interpersonal Relationships, Robert Lucas.
2. Albert Mehrabian, "Communication Without Words," Psychology Today 2 September 1968
3. Effective Interpersonal Relationships, Robert Lucas
4. Effective Interpersonal Relationships, Robert Lucas

Realize your insufficiency without God and your capabilities with God

Mapping It All Out

Classic intelligence can be defined as what is measured by the IQ tests. These tests are about logical reasoning abilities, analytical and language skills, etc. Emotional intelligence became the phrase when people began to see that human beings with a high IQ score were still failing in everyday concrete situations, whereas others with an average IQ succeeded. Emotional intelligence is another term to name our non-rational way of thinking and being. All too often, it seems that people lack determination when they need it most or lose control over their emotions in difficult situations.

As Jeanne Segal, Ph.D. points out in her book, *Raising Your Emotional Intelligence, A Practical Guide*; emotions and intellect are two halves of a whole. She goes on to explain in her book that the term EQ describes the intelligence of the heart. [1]

The root word of emotion is Latin, *motere*, which means 'to move'. Our emotions remove us from nothingness, from passiveness and motivate us to act. The more passionate we are about something, the more we are apt to act upon it.

Studies have shown that we will remember more fervently, the events in our lives that moved us the most emotionally. [2]

If the issues of the heart are anger and unforgiveness, we can close ourselves off from emotional significance towards any situation and action, often times having a hard time acting to the promises that we said we would do.

Anger wells up inside of us, ready to explode and usually at a person that is not the cause of our anger. We are usually the cause of our anger, we are usually angry at ourselves, which gets displaced on our children, spouse, coworkers, pastor or parents.

God gave us emotions and emotions are a healthy part of life. He did not create us as non-feeling mannequin type people. Yeshua became angry at the moneychangers. God was wrath towards His people. Moses lost his temper and hit the rock. Yeshua wept over Jerusalem and Lazarus. David was afraid, felt anger and was also full of joy. He also experienced lust and greed and covetousness to such desires that he skillfully took the life and the wife of a soldier. Peter had fear and Paul had grief. Emotions are not bad; they are necessary; they are an inherited gift from The Father, making His people, each one unique.

It is necessary for your mind, body, heart and soul to feel the feelings when they occur. What is unhealthy is to explode in rage without first contemplating upon why we are angry and then get control of that anger.

The other day, we were speaking with a man about anger. He gave such a great definition of his walk with bitterness and anger. He said that we must learn to identify it, resist it and reverse it. (I'm angry, I realize it, I walk out of the room, breathe, pray, come back into the room and not be angry, but be forgiving, loving and listen. All of these are my choice. I can remain in an angry state, or I can arrest it and reverse it.) Resist and reverse.

A huge part of the process is confessing. Pastor Jay teaches that the Hebrew meaning of confession is not just enough speaking the confession, but it is casting it away as in the physical lesson of the two goats in Leviticus 16. We bring it to recognition and then cast it down. Acknowledge, resist and reverse.

When Saul threw the spear, was it just anger that drove him to such lengths? Or was it jealousy, deep within? Jealousy was the channel that let loose the anger towards David.

Our mind and body are inseparable and operate as one single system. What will affect one affects the other and vice versa. Some people can go through a horrific crisis and emerge unscathed, while another will shrink into depression after just a trivial matter.

Every action that we do will bring us the like reaction back. What we sow is truly what we reap. If we choose actions that bring joy and peace to others, we will receive the like back. *"And the fruit of righteousness is sown in peace by those who make peace."* James *Ya'aqob* 3:18. *"The wrong one earns false wages, but the one sowing righteousness, a true reward."* Proverbs *Mishle'* 11:18.

Since emotion and body are one then if we are depressed, we may slump, if we are in a rage our heart races and if we are miserable, fatigue may set in. It reasons then, that emotions can and will either make us healthy or sick. Illness can take the place of an emotional reaction. Whether you find stress, anger or fear as the underlying emotion, physical symptoms are often a sign of dis-stress or dis-ease. [3,4]

- Anger is being associated with heart disease and high blood pressure. Strokes are being linked to repressed anger.

- Sadness is associated with depression, low energy levels and lower immune systems.
- Fear is being associated with allergies and overactive immune responses.
- Guilt is being associated with the side effects that a person feels guilty about.
- Shame is being associated with skin problems.
- Conflict is being associated with cancers. [5]
- Regret is being associated with Alzheimer's disease.
- Control is being associated with Parkinson's disease.
- Disgust is being associated with obsessive-compulsive disorders.

Listening to our body's messages and searching for the meanings is something that will only have a positive outcome for us. If we ignore messages that our bodies are sending us, we only create our own constant confusion, chaos, sickness and peril.

The Map

"The map is not the territory, but if correct enough, it will have a structure that is similar to the territory, which explains why we find the map useful."[6]

Alfred Korzybeski wanted to point out the difference between the sentences we utter and the experience behind the utterance. Just like maps won't show us where the next traffic jam is, our sentences don't always show us the issues we are dealing with.

Often times, when we observe reality, we filter the reality and make out our own map of this reality. This map isn't the reality. However, people often confuse their thinking, their map, with the reality it is based upon. Often times we may distort our map by placing blame on our surroundings or things that we cannot control. For example, the short winter days are often blamed for people being depressed. The gloomy skies and shoveling snow through March can bring on depression in some people. We also may blame others for our anger as in the statement: 'Oh, when they do that it makes me so mad!'

Emotions are directly linked to our experiences of life, and how we interpret life. Emotions are also directly linked to our character traits, which are results of the issues of our heart and our soul. A person who is excited may get a tight stomach, just as another person who is in complete fear. Both will experience the same tightening of the stomach, sweating of the hands and shaking, but the reasons for the reactions are different.

Think of how our bodies react to our anger. Flushed skin, heart racing, and cramping of muscles can all be symptoms of anger. Now think of how our bodies react to a hug from our spouse, or a soft kind word. Isn't it calming? Our heart relaxes and we can almost feel tension melt away.

"A soft answer turns away wrath, but a harsh word stirs up strife." Proverbs *Mishle'* 15:1

"A word spoken at the right time is like apples of gold in settings of silver." Proverbs *Mishle'* 25:11

Thus, it is through Mussar that we can learn to define what our bodies are telling us. We can learn to listen and become aware of the process of tuning into our emotions and character traits. We can redefine our paths.

1. Raising Your Emotional Intelligence, Jeanne Segal, Ph.D.
2. Raising Your Emotional Intelligence, Jeanne Segal, Ph.D.
3. 7 Steps to Emotional Intelligence, Patrick E. Merlevede, M.Sc.
4. Rabbi Messer also teaches that dis-ease is related to stress, being not in alignment with The Father and His Torah, Simchat Torah Beit Midrash, Denver CO
5. A German doctor, Ryke Goerd Hamer, M.D. carried out a survey in the 1980's about cancer, discovering that the type of cancer people had was related to the type of conflict in their lives.
6. Alfred Korzybski, Science and Sanity, Lakeville Conn. Institute of General Semantics

People are attracted to enthusiasm

What is Mussar

Mussar. A small word with not much flamboyance. Just a word. But it's meaning in Hebrew is rich and life changing. The word Mussar means correction, instruction and in modern Hebrew means ethics. That's what the *word* means. But it is a way of life, a path of life, a direction, a change of life. It is one that our Messiah taught, lived, and breathed. Yeshua was able to rise above the hate that was so prolific towards Him. He taught His disciples the same when He told Peter, *Kepha*, to put the sword down. He was Mussar before there was Mussar. The true ethics of life, the true Walk then comes from Yeshua which comes from The Father, *HaShem, Adonai, Elohim, YHWH*. And what is His Walk? It is His character, His lifestyle, His principles, The Torah.

Mussar became a movement in the second half of the nineteenth century under Rabbi Yisrael Lipkin Salanter. Roots of Mussar go back to the tenth century Babylonia when sage Sa'adia Ga'on published a book titled *Book of Beliefs and Opinions*. There is a chapter in the book; How A Person Ought To Behave In The World; which started the wheels in progress in the Jewish world about human nature. A disciple of Rabbi Salanter, Rabbi Simcha Zissel Ziv founded a yeshiva in Kelm, a Lithuanian town, which became the point of Kelm Mussar. Rabbi Noson Tzvi Finkel of Slabodka and Rabbi Yosef Yozel Hurwitz of Novarodok also founded yeshivas and started their own teachings of Mussar. [1]

Kelm Mussar emphasizes the powers of the mind, his motto was: "Take time, be exact and unclutter the mind." Slabodka Mussar is more behavioral, to conduct oneself with people who really believe that they are made in the image of God. The Slabodka motto is "the majesty of man." Novarodok Mussar is the more radical, more aggressive for change. The motto: "Storm the soul." [2]

Modern day Mussar teachers draw on all three versions as well as other sources. When I studied a course in Mussar, read some of the books, and continue to study, I saw the Messiah, Yeshua, through and through in these teachings of Mussar. He is interwoven amongst the pages of The Bible, from Genesis to Revelation, and interwoven in great teachings and lessons. He was the ultimate Teacher, He was the perfect example. He is the perfect Teacher, Rabbi, Mentor, Example and our very Life.

Mussar is not a study intended to be practiced in isolation or away from other people. If we limit our spread of life to be around people just like us, we miss the whole point in having others involved. Yet, we must at times separate ourselves from the world, but only for periods of contemplation. More value is actually placed on refining the inner resources that will allow us to carry on in the middle of the busy market place, but with the kind of inner strength and insight that will render us resistant to the powerful temptations society inevitably sends our way. [3]

There is a Hebrew way to study the Scriptures. The acronym is PARDES, meaning: Parasha, Ramez, Drash and Sod. In the type of studying, *ramez,* we are taught to look forward, to find the Scripture back. And look back to find the Scripture forward. Yeshua was constantly doing this and teaching in this way. Yeshua/Jesus draws from the past to give to the present to offer for the new and beyond. I see this also in the Mussar teachings, going back in Scripture to go forward.

Too often we draw only upon our past. But God is walking before us, in our presence, and as Paul Wilbur sings: "In Your Presence, that's where I belong…" So, it is a two fold journey. We have to keep moving forward. The soul is not stagnant; we are always on a journey. Our soul craves to be the likeness of God, and to be near Him. Our soul is not motionless in this life we have to live.

Mussar was almost lost when so many of the practitioners and students were killed in the Holocaust. In the late nineteenth and early twentieth centuries, Mussar was on a path that led away from the main of the Jewish Community. Yet Mussar did not die, it has always been with us, in the Jewish Community and the Christian Community. Some have been gifted with the teachings of Mussar and don't even know they are following it, let alone teaching it.

Mussar teaches that there are gates. They often name the chapters in the books 'gates' and refer to soul traits as gates to the soul. There is the gate of anger, the gate of joy and so on. Lucifer went through the gate of jealousy.

When we work on our character traits, we can see which gate we have or have not entered and we open our hearts allowing the Spirit to work within us. This improvement is called *tikkun ha' middot* – improving the traits of character. In Alan Morinis' book *Climbing Jacobs Ladder,* he quotes Rabbi Perr in regards to The Father telling us to circumcise our hearts. In Jeremiah 31:31 and Hebrews 8 we read that we are to circumcise our hearts, it is the *Tanakh* and the *Brit Chadasha* saying the same thing. .

Rabbi Perr reminds us all that we are told to circumcise our hearts because we are so closed.

Mussar, to simplify the issue teaches that there are three aspects to the soul, but not different anatomical parts.[4]

The inner element called *neshama*, is fundamentally holy and pure. It is the image of the soul in which man was created, in the image of God. Because this inner image of the soul is The Likeness of God, it is incorruptible. Some say that it is divine and joined to the divine.

The disciples were always asking Yeshua to show them God. He would explain to them that He and The Father are one. He was showing His Apostles that He was the image and the likeness of The Father. He taught them to observe what He did, to watch how He behaved, and most important, to see who He glorified. That He was/is the *neshama*.

Yet, we are a physical people. We need something to 'see'. People need an image, a visual, a starting point. We have the *mezuzah* and *tzits tzits*, things we can see. But YHWH is all, the beginning and the end. The Alef and the Tav. He was there before there was. So, can I be an image of the Love of God?

There is a difference between the image and the likeness. One is a choice, the other is not. You did not choose your *neshama*. God is spirit, a breath and we are an extension of that breath.

The likeness is something of a choice. The behavioral part of a being. We can choose to behave as Yeshua did/does or we can choose to behave in our own humanly realm which Rabbi Shau'l (Paul) refers to as our flesh.

Another fundamental Mussar truth is that we can choose to do good because we are given free will.[5] Why then, if we all have a choice, and we are made in the image and likeness of God, why is evil present in our lives? Why do we say unkind words? Mussar teaches that awareness is one of the first responses to the *yetzer ha'ra*, the evil inclination. When we are not aware of our responses to situations, and are not aware of our reactions to actions then we end up in emotional stress, not dealing with the situation at all but allowing our own self of ego to govern our very actions.

The second realm of the soul is called the *ruach*, which translates into Spirit. It is our spirit of life, our reactions given to us by the Great Comforter, Yeshua.

The third realm of the soul is *nefesh* and it is the most noticeable and reachable to us. It is the aspect of our very being that will display our character traits, our anger, joy, worry and love. This element of the soul registers the good or the bad that we do in our lives.

Mussar can be summarized as *tikkum middot ha'nefesh* — improving the traits of the soul.

The Talmud seeks the secret of the longevity of the Sages, but the answers never involve diet or other physical aspects of one's life style; it is obvious to the Sages that physical existence is dependent on the spiritual health.

R'Dosaben Harkinos, who lived to a very old age, (Yevamos 16a) is the fitting presenter for this reality. It is not the pampering of the body which assures long life, but rather the development of the soul *(Derech Avos)*.

This is where we get the wholeness that we are supposed to be. Do you ever feel disconnected to a person? To God? At the age of 19, my son wrote a very profound song, referring to young people and The Father. He used words like; 'disconnected' and 'away from'. Don't we often feel that way? But God did not move from us, we have moved from Him. To be the whole person that He created that is our goal. When we are off in our connecting with Him, our wholeness is fractured.

In Hebrew the combined word for all the traits of the *nefesh* — soul is *middot*. 'Traits of Character' is the English plural term that *nefesh* is translated into. But the Hebrew word, *middot,* which is singular, literally means 'measures.' When we think of our character and soul traits in measures, it gives logic to our understanding why we behave in a certain manner. It is the amount, the measure of anger that we have, or the amount, the measure of patience that we contain.

In the book, *Everyday Holiness, The Path to Mussar,* Alan Morinis tells us what Rabbi Yisrael Salanter termed the three stages of Mussar. To understand these statements and tie them in with Yeshua is crucial as believers in our voyage as we start this journey.

The first stage is sensitivity. Being aware of our actions and reactions and feelings before they sprout. Why am I feeling this way? What brought me full circle from a peaceful moment to anger or impatience or moodiness? What triggered me?

When the adulteress was brought before Jesus/Yeshua in the crowd, He did not run to her screaming, or run to the men holding her, or wave His hands in the air. He was quiet and calm and understanding. He was silent for a time.

We know that it happened for The Glory of God and to proclaim Yeshua as Savior, but, the actions of the men, what did they represent? Was there jealousy maybe of Jesus? Maybe there was anger that He was saying who He was? Maybe there was a pit in their stomach that they were losing their control. Jesus responded by writing in the sand and then by suggesting that whoever was perfect to throw the first stone.

Sensitivity is a thought process, a power that we have to analyze at the moment.

The second stage listed is self-restraint. This level takes it from a thought to a verb, an action. Now that I've realized why I am feeling my blood pressure rise, and that unmistakable crease in my forehead is forming, I am about to lose my patience. Self–restraint is my thought process through prayer, that I regain control of the situation and my reaction. *Help me Yeshua not to lose my patience; You take control of this situation. Breathe...*

I can claim dominion over the situation at hand through Christ. This goes deep into our soul, which Mussar is all about. It is a transfiguration of our actions and reactions which means exercising our will, our free choice to react or to not react.

None had greater self-restraint than our Messiah. He is the example we shoot for. His calmness is first made known to us when He was twelve. His parents were madly looking for Him, and they were probably in a panic. Have you ever briefly misplaced your child? I can visualize the scene: They ran up to him, eyes wide, probably breathing hard, and questioning Him. Where have you been? We were worried sick! Don't ever do this to us again!

What were His actions? Did he yell at them, or cry, or whine, or beg for no punishment? No, He calmly told them that He was about His Fathers' business.

The third stage is transformation. This third stage can come rather easy if you first recognize the first stage. We can't have transformation without sensitivity. Proverbs states that out of the abundance of the heart the mouth does speak. Grab a hold of that Proverb first, and the transformation will happen. Acknowledge, resist and reverse.

Transformation deals with truth and untruth, in ourselves and how we are receiving a message.

Has anyone ever said to you: 'what have you done with your hair?' Where does that statement take you?

I may like my hair, and she doesn't. The words aren't truth, they are opinion. The truth comes from my inner soul on how I perceive this statement and deal with it. It is sensitivity to my feelings, the heart; self-restraint to what my mouth wants to spout off, and the transformation.

Yeshua was always dealing in truths for He is the Truth. He never gave us permission to: 'well, if you feel this then do this…go with your feelings…go with your heart, hey, go with the flow.' No, He never gave us the go ahead to lie to ourselves, to tell us that we have a right to feel this way.

"*Meanwhile, the high priest questioned Jesus about His disciples and His teaching. "I have spoken openly to the world," Jesus replied. "I always taught in synagogues or at the temple, where all the Jews come together. I said nothing in secret. Why question me? Ask those who heard me. Surely they know what I said." When Jesus said this, one of the officials nearby struck Him in the face. "Is this the way you answer the high priest?" he demanded. "If I said something wrong," Jesus replied, "testify as to what is wrong. But if I spoke the truth, why did you strike me?" Then Annas sent Him, still bound to Caiaphas the high priest.*" John 18:19-24 NIV

Yeshua answers the interrogation by explaining that He spoke truth. Truth is a synonym for Yeshua.

Rabbi Sha'ul, Paul, tells us that we are a new creature, a new beginning in The Messiah. This is where our transformation comes from, The Holy Spirit. It is the allowing of the Holy Spirit, the *Ruach haKodesh* working in me. We are not to beat ourselves up in acts of unforgiveness. Mussar teaches just the opposite, yet not to bury our heads like the ostrich, but deal with our soul traits, encouraging each other along the way of restoration.

Connecting

Connecting to a source is imperative in anything we do. Electricity must connect with a source. Love connects with a source. Mussar connects with *the* source: *Elohim*, God, *Adonai*, YHWH. He is our source, our connecting point. When we falter from Him, when we stray from The Source, we lose our way, our balance, and our direction. We lose the teachings, the guidance. We lose the very source that Yeshua/Jesus drew off of. The very source that He was. *That He is.* When we go off on our own, our own direction, our own path, we die a spiritual death and most of the time don't even know it. The Torah through the Spirit is our Source.

Rabbi Messer teaches that three things can kill us in a spiritual, emotional, financial, and maybe even a physical sense. These three things are religion, ownership and dependence. [6]

We cannot correct our selves or our character traits if we have no source, no connecting point, no beginning, and no end. We are random beings, trying to live right, reading the writings of Yeshua/Jesus, knowing we *should* behave like that, but we struggle, and worse, give up. Mussar training brings us full circle back to the Scriptures, back to our Messiah, back to Torah, back to The Source, YHWH, God.

But to fully understand our Source, one must look at life, the Bible and actually us with a Hebrew mindset. Mussar is Jewish, a Jewish teaching coming from learned and wise Rabbis' and a Jewish way of life. And the Jewish came from Judah, which came from Abraham, The Hebrew, which came from our source, YHWH.

In the movie, *Prince of Egypt*, Moshe is dancing with his father-in-law to be and he sings a song to Moshe about looking at life through Heavens' Eyes. If you really think about those two words, Heavens' Eyes, what is that? It is our source, YHWH, Elohim, Adonai, God. It is Yeshua/Jesus, Israelite, Moadim, Torah, Shabbats, Love, Grace, Deliverance, Salvation, Redemption, Shalom, Hebrew, through and through.

So, as Rabbi Messer of Simchat Torah Beit Midrash teaches, please take off your Hellenistic glasses and look at life with a Hebrew mindset.

1. Everyday Holiness, The Path to Mussar Alan Morinis
2. Everyday Holiness, The Path to Mussar Alan Morinis
3. Climbing Jacobs Ladder, Alan Morinis
4. Climbing Jacobs Ladder, Alan Morinis
5. Climbing Jacobs Ladder, Alan Morinis
6. Simchat Torah Beit Midrash Denver CO, Rabbi Ralph Messer

You can't control the length of your life, but you can control its width and depth

The Purpose of Living

Az past nisht is Yiddish for 'that doesn't suit you'. It is my favorite saying, and set of code of words that I learned in the Mussar teachings.[1] I repeat it to my self and to my children. Whatever is in control of me at the moment, if it is not The Presence of God, it does not suit me. *Az past nisht.*

Is the purpose of life is to have a big home, a great job, an even better career, a college degree, lots and lots of money, good insurance, a fancy car that is paid off, beautiful hair, a great body, great muscles, the smartest kid, the prettiest kid, the fastest kid, the happiest kid, the best big screen TV, an ipod, a cell phone, your credit card paid off, a smart dog, a hot cup of coffee, a beautiful wife, a buff husband or if that doesn't work, a good divorce lawyer.

Is the purpose of life is to run yourself ragged at church, join this, volunteer for that, pay for this, sing that, parade for this.

Or is the purpose of life is to do good *mitzvohs,* deeds with your right hand, help this organization, pay for that orphanage, send this child to school, all while the left hand is cheating this company, that person, and even the government. Just don't get caught.

Maybe the purpose of life is to have the biggest church or even belong to the biggest church or to have the best seat in the biggest church. Or, the purpose in life is to do the feast days and Shabbat but argue with your husband/wife and snap at your kids all the way to synagogue, or argue all the way to church, then smile at everyone. So, the purpose of life is to be happy! And if you're not – fake it.

Really? That sounds Hellenistic to me.

"I don't care what my child does; I just want him/her to be happy." I have said that so many times. "I don't care if my child is a trash collector, or a doctor, I just want him/her to be happy."

But, we are to be a Holy people, a set apart nation, and a set apart people. We should raise ourselves and our children to be Holy. We are a set apart people through the blood of The Messiah, but we need to behave like Him. *"Be Holy for I YHWH your Elohim am Holy."* Leviticus *Wayyiqra* 19:2. *"Do you not know that you are a Dwelling Place of Elohim and that the Spirit of Elohim dwells in you? If anyone destroys the Dwelling Place of*

Elohim, Elohim shall destroy him. For the Dwelling Place of Elohim is set-apart, which you are." 1Corinthians 3:16, 17.

Being holy is a gift from God. It is a free gift. Can you make yourself holy? Can you arrive at your 'holiness' by your works? If that would be true, then one might be more 'holier' than another. And depending on the 'religion' one religion might consider that they are more 'holier' than the other religion. Is it by what they wear? Is it by what they do not wear? Is it by the religious methods that they do? Or don't do? The holiness that we are, that we become is strictly from Yeshua and The Father. It is already there. We simply need to *behave* that way. Being greedy or yelling at your spouse or cursing at a hammer because you smashed your thumb, or gossiping is not behaving 'holy'.

Pirkei Avos, The Ethics of the Fathers [2], teaches that man was set on this earth to fulfill God's will. Since we owe Him everything, we deserve no thanks for anything we do at His behalf.

Israel is a set apart nation. We are His people, He is our God. But how to behave? It's not easy. He was/is without sin, He had no baggage, no skeletons in the closet, no abuse factors, no issues of the heart, no idols of the heart and no generational curses. Nevertheless -we do.

The purpose of life for a believer of Yeshua and the Torah should be different. It should be unlike that of the world. But what is the world? What are worldly things? We may think that they are physical things; we may assume that they are dress, or makeup or books, or school or whatever we judge 'worldly.' But the Scriptures speak of a world that is outside of God's realm and outside His Spirit. It is outside of God's Ways. It is literally outside of God's camp.

The Torah, God's teaching and instruction will keep us in God's world, in His realm and in His camp.

"Having purposed it, He brought us forth by the Word of Truth, for us to be a kind of first fruits of His creatures. So, then, my beloved brothers, let every man be swift to hear, slow to speak, slow to wrath, for the wrath of man does not work the righteousness of Elohim." James Ya'aqob 1:18-20. *"But the fruit of the Spirit is love, joy, peace, patience, kindness, goodness, trusting, worthiness, gentleness, self control. Against such there is no law."* Galatians 5:22,23.

We have to first acknowledge that we have to correct a few things, maybe one thing, maybe several, to be different, to be peculiar, and to be set apart. We need to be that light, that pillar of salt. *"You are the salt of the earth, but if the salt becomes tasteless, how shall it be seasoned? For it is no longer of any use but to be thrown out and to be trodden down by men."* Matthew *Mattityahu*, 5:13.

One major purpose of life for a believer is to have joy. But it is not a joy in ourselves, or our house, or children, or job or our money. It is joy in The Messiah which will glorify our Father in Heaven. *"But be glad and rejoice forever in what I create; for look, I create Yerushalayim a rejoicing and her people a joy. And I shall rejoice in Yerushalayim, and shall joy in My people and let the voice of weeping no more be heard in her, nor the voice of crying."* Isaiah *Yeshayahu* 65:18.

"And my soul shall be joyful in the Lord; it shall rejoice in His salvation." Psalms *Tehillim*, 35:9.

"....And truly our fellowship is with the Father and with His Son Yeshua, The Messiah. And we write this to you in order that your joy might be complete." 1John *Yohanan*, 1:3b, 4.

When we try to find joy in the world and not in Him; that is where we confuse our Holiness with our happiness. "Oh, if only I was happy.... You don't make me happy anymore...I wish I was happy." If we seek to be Holy, seek The Kingdom first, then the illumination of His joy will enter into our very souls.

Baggage, bad attitudes, anger, lack of patience, and fear, will take away any joy for we are locked in the mindset of 'happiness'. Any judgmental attitudes will take away all joy and that's a promise. We can learn, through The Messiah, and by putting the works of Mussar in our lives, to retain that joy, or for some to acquire it for the first time.

If you have crooked teeth, you might seek an orthodontist, if you are near sighted, you would seek an eye doctor. Frizzy hair? Go to a stylist. Out of shape? Exercise. Ugly fingernails? Paint them. Thin lips? Botox. Wrinkles? Cream. And on and on it goes...for the outside of our souls.

Let's work on our insides. Let's work on our heart.

"Watch over your heart with all diligence. For out of it are the sources of life." Proverbs *Mishle'* 4:23

Isn't that very interesting that we are told that in our hearts are the sources of life and we are to guard our heart. Right before that, King Solomon writes that his father, King David told him to have his heart hold fast his words, Proverbs 4:4

Our hearts are to be wise, hold fast the commandments of God, and not be haughty or proud. Our hearts are called wicked, and we are told that out of our mouths the heart does speak, Luke 6:45.

The Heart

We are told that the heart of the wise gives our tongues discretion, Proverbs 16:23. We are told not to let our hearts be troubled, John 14:1 and not to judge in our hearts, Romans 10:6. Hearts can be hardened by us or by God. Yet we are told not to harden our hearts. We are to stand steadfast in our hearts, make melody to The Lord in our hearts, and have the peace of God rule in our hearts. The Torah is to be written upon our hearts, and The Messiah may dwell in our hearts by faith, Ephesians 3:17. And we are to Praise The Lord and Love The Lord with all our hearts.

The word heart in the English language is heart. Don't we either think of a red shaped item on greeting cards like the ones we drew in kindergarten? Or we think literal, of our heart, pumping continuously in our bodies.

In the Hebrew language however, heart can take many forms. It means literal heart, *leb, bal, lebab, or libbah*. It can mean soul, or breath: *Nephesh*, from Strongs 5314, *naphash*, to be breathed upon. (Exodus *Shemoth* 23:9, Leviticus *Wayyiqra* 26:16, Deuteronomy *Devarim* 24:15, 1Samuel *1Shemu'el* 2:33 Proverbs *Mishle'* 23:7, 28:25, Lamentations *Ekah* 3:51, Ezekiel *Yehezqel* 25:15, 27:31, and Hosea *Hoshea* 4:8).

It can mean covered part, *sekvi*, as in Job *Iyob* 38:36. It means bowels, *meim* in Psalms *Tehillim* 40:8. And it means centered, midst, *qereb*, in Jeremiah *Yirmeyahu*. 9:8.

In the book *Climbing Jacobs Ladder*, Alan Morinis teaches that another well-used term in Mussar is the Yiddish word *derherin*. *Her* means to hear and *derher* means that you hear something that makes a difference in your life. You can hear a baby cry, but until you have had a baby and have held it while it cries, or go to her as she cries in distress, the sound of a baby crying means nothing other than a baby crying. Ask any nursing mommy; the sound of a baby crying can and often will completely change her physically at that moment.

Our heart will be a determining factor in our lives, in our habits and in our walk. If we have any issues of the heart it will block our path to peace. We can *do* all the things we are supposed to do. We can read all the things we are to read, and study all the things we are to study. But, 'we never act on what we study; we act on what's in our heart'. [3] 'God will use your mind and your mouth to show you what is in your heart'. [4]

Man has five faculties. They are hearing, sight, taste, smell and touch. They encompass all of mans actions and no act can be performed with out at least one of them. The heart acts through them, as these five faculties transmit to the heart. The heart is the center of these actions, reactions and feelings. *The Ways of The Tzaddikim.*

If there are issues in our hearts, certain character traits will rise above the others.

Please take some soul-searching time to discover any issues in your heart. Is there anger towards a parent? Are you unforgiving of a wrong? Are you stingy, or fearful of life? Do you lose your patience easily with your children? These are the results of issues of the heart. But God has promised us a better way, a better life. But just like making an appointment with the dentist and actually *going,* we need to actually deal with our hearts, souls, character traits and habits.

The purpose of living? To be a holy people, glorifying The Father in all we do, complete with joy! His joy!

We were not made to be in our esteem. We were created by a Creator for His esteem. *"Since you were precious in My eyes, you have been esteemed, and I have loved you. And I give men in your place, and peoples for your life. Do not fear, for I am with you, I shall bring your seed from the east, and gather you from the west. I shall say to the north, 'Give them up!' And to the south, 'Do not keep them back!' Bring My sons from afar, and My daughters from the ends of the earth, all those who are called by My Name, whom I have created, formed, even made for My esteem."* Isaiah *Yeshayahu* 43:4-7

There is a purpose that gets white washed with time, cultures, economics, trauma, crisis, life, and death. That purpose gets lost in our denominations, our religions and our own perception of what we perceive the Bible to say.

His purpose gets transliterated amongst our friends and family with their ever well intentioned advice. 'Thus saith The Lord….for your life…". Have you ever heard that? Have you ever said that?

Recently, I explained to a friend of mine to stop searching for His Will out there. You won't find it out there. His will for His people is in the Bible.

Is His will that you dabble in witchcraft? No. Is His will that you eat pork? No. Is it His will that you forget His *Moadim* and partake in other types of holidays? No. Is it His will for you to get involved with pornography, or divorce, or abuse, or mistrust, or lie or cheat, or forget the Sabbath? No, no and no.

"For Elohim did not call us to uncleanness but in set-apartness." 1Thessalonians 4:7

We are the residence of the living God, the Ruach HaKodesh, The Holy Spirit. We are merely the caretakers; we are not the owners or the Master, yet merely the vessel to live out His Will. But when we come to believe that we own the residence then our agenda becomes the agenda and we loose the perception of what is His Will for us. What is His purpose? When I hear the words: 'The purpose of life', I can very easily translate that in my brain to mean, what is the purpose of my life for me. Hmmmm, what am I here for, what would I like to do. What do I enjoy, what is my pleasure? The focus turns around me, me and me.

When I take my eyes off of the Master YHWH and view life through my eyes, I loose focus that I am merely the caretaker of the temple and not the dweller or the master. I begin to see things through clouded eyes and focus on what I have or don't have.[5]

"And the Elohim of Peace Himself set you completely apart and your entire being and spirit and body – be preserved blameless at the coming of Our Master Yeshua Messiah." 1Thessalonains 5:23

I'm here to encourage you. You can change your life, and live the purpose God has intended for you. Remember that God is the place of the universe but the universe does not contain God. His purpose is all that matters.

1. Every Day Holiness, The Path of Mussar, Alan Morinis
2. Pirkei Avos, The Ethics of The Fathers, Mesorah Publications
3. Rabbi Ralph Messer, Simchat Torah Beit Midrash Denver CO
4. Rabbi Ralph Messer, Simchat Torah Beit Midrash Denver CO
5. Rabbi Michael Shapiro, Scottsdale Torah Institute, Phoenix AZ

When you lose yourself in God's purpose only then will you fully live

Our Generational Curses

"Curses? I don't have any curses…"

We heard that statement at a church we were visiting after Pastor Jay was trying to explain about generational curses. Some people seem to think that the curses spoke of are put on us by witches in black pointy hats and green noses with big, hairy moles and long thin fingernails.

"And it shall be if you do not obey the voice of The Lord your Elohim, to guard to do all His commands and His law which I command you today, that all these curses shall come upon you and overtake you:

"Cursed are you in the city, and cursed are you in the field.

"Cursed is your basket and your kneading bowl.

"Cursed is the fruit of your body and the fruit of your land, the increase of your cattle and the offspring of your flocks.

"Cursed are you when you come in and cursed are you when you go out.

"The Lord sends on you the curse, the confusion and the rebuke in all that you set your hand to do until you are destroyed and until you perish quickly because of the evil of your doings by which you have forsaken Me.

"The Lord makes the plague cling to you until He has consumed you from the land which you are going to possess.

"The Lord smites you with wasting disease, and with inflammation, and with burning, and with extreme heat and with the sword, and with blight and with mildew. And they shall pursue you until you perish." Deuteronomy *Debarim* 28:15-23

"The Lord shall smite you with the boils of Egypt, with tumors, with the scab and with the itch, from which you are unable to be healed.

"The Lord shall smite you with madness and blindness and bewilderment of heart.

"And you shall be groping at noon, as a blind man gropes in darkness, and not prosper in your ways. And you shall be only oppressed and plundered all the days with no one to save you." Deuteronomy *Debarim*. 28:27-30

What is important to realize in these verses is that YHWH puts the curse on us. It is not a curse from hasatan, it is a direct consequence of our or our forefathers disobedience. We have been separated from The Father for a time, but as we learn to walk within the boundaries of Torah, we lessen that separation and discover the generational conditions that may plague us. We can not walk the walk of YHWH without instruction – otherwise we make up our own instruction.

Let's look at the parallels of curses and blessings.

Curses	Blessings
With a cause: Proverbs 26:2	Genesis 22:17
Generational: Deuteronomy 28	Exodus 32:29
Witchcraft: Galatians 3	Deuteronomy 30:19
Apostasy: Galatians 1:6-9	Nehemiah 13:2
	Psalms 24:5

Being immersed into Yeshua we now have the power of the Holy Spirit to bring awareness and overcome these generational curses.

There are some ailments, some things in life that we can never change. Breast cancer runs in my lineage, yet I am sure that part of the reason for my breast cancer was the disobedience that I was living in as a twenty year old, including abortions and birth control pills. Even though years later, I repented and stepped into the saving grace of Yeshua, I had consequences coming my way.

Why is it that if someone murders, yet repents and becomes a Christian, we still expect that person to pay the consequences for his actions of murder – ultimately prison? We are grateful that now he is a believer, but I don't think anyone would succumb to the idea that he should not suffer consequences for his actions and not go to prison. But – when we become ill, cancer, we pray for healing, (which we *are* healed by His stripes) yet somehow we do not want to suffer the consequences of our prior actions/disobedience. There are things in life we can not control, or stop. There are things in life we can not change and things in life we can not answer.

Within the verses of Deuteronomy 28 we see the following curses that may come upon us for lack of obedience.

- Mental illness or emotional breakdowns
- A persistent or repeated sickness
- To be barren, a propensity to miscarry
- Divorce and collapse of the family and marriage
- Financial problems/lack and decrease
- Accidents and being prone to accidents
- Suicides and early/unnatural deaths

- Unforgiveness and bitter root judgments
- Self Imposed Curses

This list mainly concerns the realm of the physical and can sound quite intimidating. But just think for a moment about what the medical community calls our physical histories. Both sides of my family have had cancer, so subsequently could it be that is the reason that I got breast cancer? My college life style also contributed, (i.e. birth control pills and abortion) which would create great consequences. My father died when he was 48, and I was diagnosed at 48 and The Lord brought me through the cancer and all the treatments.

Our forefathers moved away from God's teaching and instruction as it was prophesized. So now, we teach our children about these generational curses, about our DNA.

The physical generational curses are easy to see, cancer, heart problems, weight, anorexia, diabetes, etc. It's the inside ones we don't expel, or talk about. We like to hide them.

I had no problem asking people to pray for me as I was going through cancer. I had no problems explaining the cancer histories in my family. I had no problems discussing this with my children. I had no problems admitting that cancer is coming from my side of the family.

But a short temper issue? Me? No way. When my husband would comment on my short temper, I would fly into denial. Why was it that I could ask a friend to pray for me while I diet, but it is so hard to ask her to pray for me as I work on my short temper?

Why is it that we get so defensive when it is a character trait?

My dad had a very short temper. Did that make him bad? No, his dad probably had a short temper. I have a short temper, as do my sister and brother. Okay, so we have short tempers. We obtained that character trait from our biological father's generations. There is absolutely no blame whatsoever, we are simply bringing it to recognition and now let's deal with it.

We should look at our character traits as something we may need to work on. Just like a person who needs glasses, they need help seeing. There is nothing wrong or scary about that.

While working on this book, my nine year old son and I went to Phoenix to be with my 89 year old mother. The second day we were there; she sat in the sun too long, (diagnoses was also dehydration), came into the house and proceeded to pass out and hit her head on the stairs. By the time

I ran to the front where my son was riding his bike and back into the house to call 911 the blood from the head wound was visible. The paramedics came; she was taken to the ER and released late that afternoon.

But, in that interim, I recognized a huge character trait.

When my father collapsed just moments before his death, my mother snapped at me to wait outside for the paramedics. Her tone and voice frightened me. I was nine. I snapped the exact same way at my nine year old when my mother collapsed. It was spooky.

How about anger issues? Fear? Patience? Trust? Do any of these give issue to you? Some may be coming from genes and some traits develop from issues of the heart.

Only you know your issues. Only you know your character traits. Only you know the areas in your life that you wish were somewhat better, a little better or just might need a big fix.

Rabbi Messer teaches that you don't decide your future, you decide your habits and your habits decide your future. [1]

The Ba'al Shem Tov, the master of the Chasidic Movement was forever correcting himself as a good character would. He was always checking his vision, is it of the Master? Or is it of him.

Our question or answer is not about fault, blame or accusations. If we place fault or blame on ourselves or someone else, then the problem becomes external rather than internal. We have redirected the message coming from The Master YHWH about our inner soul to something external. Then, I can begin to view life as it is happening to me, instead of a unit of God's creation. I can then place blame as in 'they did that to me' or 'it is because of them that I…'

It takes great cultivation in our mindset to observe things happening in the world as a 'whole' instead of a 'me'. (Rabbi Shapiro, Scottsdale Torah Institute, AZ).

We try and keep our undesirable traits bottled up and hidden for no one to see. We look at ourselves in a different way than others perceive us. Yet, we have a preconceived idea of what we think we look like to others. Or a preconceived idea of what we want to look like to others. Eventually, these character traits, or issues of the heart, explode and reveal themselves as a great big pimple. It takes time for the redness to develop a white head, then it pops, there is bleeding, a scab and then healing. But depending on the size of the pimple, the size of the deviation from YHWH or the size of the deception, the healing could result in scarring. Does anyone not have scarring in their very souls?

Yitzchok Isaac Sher, Slobodka writes of habits verses character traits in the book *Cheshbon Ha-Nafesh*. He quotes The Vilna Gaon regarding the importance of correcting one's habits.

"I shall conclude with the noble words of the Vilna Gaon regarding the importance of correcting one's habits. In his commentary on the verse Proverbs 4:26, 'Straighten the circuit of your feet and all of your ways will be set', he comments:

"I have already written that there are two types of character traits, natural traits which man has from birth, and traits which one acquires through habit. The traits which man has from birth are referred to as 'his ways' for they are the ways he follows from when he was created. The traits, which are acquired, are referred to as hergel – habit (etymologically related to regal – foot) for he has habituated himself to act according to them. The habitual traits must be guarded against and "straightened". When he does so, then his natural traits will be guarded as a matter of course. This is what the verse was referring to when it stated, straighten the circuit of your feet – i.e., the bad habits which have become your traits must be straightened so that slowly but surely these negative traits are eradicated. It then becomes part of one's nature to act properly. If one does so, then all of your ways will be set – i.e., your natural traits will be set, established on a firm base (yikonu – set – being etymologically related ken – base). But if one fails to straighten his acquired traits, then his ways – his natural traits – will not be set. Character traits are like a strand of pearls; if one ties a knot at the end, then they will all remain on the strand. But if one fails to do so, then they will all be lost. This is true of character traits as well. The verse therefore tells us that if one straightens the circuit of his feet, then his ways will be set".

The Gaon was able to deduce that this verse comes to warn the righteous individuals who have managed to correct their natural character traits, that they must correct their acquired ones as well. Otherwise there will be no basis for their efforts and toil in trying to perfect themselves." Yitzchok Isaac Sher, Slobodka. [2]

Generational curses encompass transgressions and iniquities and it takes great consciousness and recognition on our part to bring these traits, to the point of recognition. It is only through that order that we may reverse them. Transgressions are to cross against God's will, it is a willful sin, a form of rebellion and pride. The iniquities are sins passed from generation to generation, they are generational sins.

In Deuteronomy 28:15, God says that the curses or the blessings will overtake us. Think on that, curses overtaking us. It is as if they are chasing us down.

Are you from a divorced family? Are you divorced? Are you from an abusive family? Are you abusive or are you in an abusive relationship? These curses, the sins of the fathers; Jeremiah 16:10; are chasing you down. And, these sins, if not recognized and renounced and reversed will chase your children down. We will enable these sins to our next generation.

The Torah, Deuteronomy 30, teaches us what life is, what His will is, what His purpose is. We are given a choice. We are taught about life and death; good and evil; and blessings and curses. Choose Life!

Recognize – Repent – Renounce – Resist – Reverse

Recognize the sin, bring it to attention.

Repent to whoever you need to ask forgiveness of. Asking forgiveness and confessing our sins is part of the process.

Renounce that sin. Don't hide it, for any secret sin will hunt us down.

Resist – turn from it. Teshuva

Reverse – replace it with the positive. Always replace, reverse, the negative with a positive. You will begin to feed the very purpose of your life.

We can do all things through The Messiah. We can worship The Father. We can love one another. We can walk in His Joy. Remember, we can straighten the circuits of our feet for God is faithful to His Blessings, too. His desire is that we Live and enjoy Him and the Life that He gave us. Let's live in His Blessings, His Life and shine His everlasting love.

(For more information on generational curses please visit Simchat haMashiach Beit Emunah www.joyinthemessiah.com shmbe@joimail.com and Simchat Torah Beit Midrash www.Torah.tv)

1. Rabbi Messer STBM, Denver CO
2. Yitzchok Isaac Sher, Slobodka, Cheshbon HaNefesh,

To achieve excellence, begin with discipline

The Battle Within

There are many stories, myths and riddles that resemble one another. One such analogy is a story about two opposites that struggle within us. It's two wolves, the good & the bad, or two dogs, one light one dark, or it is two creatures, one good one evil; depending on the culture telling the story. Yet all the stories are the same. There is a battle within us; the one that grows is the one that is fed.

These are really inner traits of the soul. Soul traits. We define them as character traits. The thread runs deep within us, and can easily be seen as generational.

We have the *yetzer ha'tov*, the impulse to do good, and the *yetzer ha'ra*, the evil inclination.

Rabbi Eliyahu Dessler identifies the *bechirah* point in all of us. *Bechirah* means choice, and links us to free will. It is that inner battle where choice is very alive at any split section.

"For the good that I wish to do, I do not do, but the evil I do not wish to do, this I practice." Romans 7:19

Even for Rabbi Sha'ul, (Paul) life was a choice and very hard at times. But he continues in his edification that through the Torah, God's teaching and instruction *and* the Holy Spirit, through the love of The Messiah that we are over comers of our flesh.

"So that the Torah truly is set apart, and the command set apart and righteous and good. Therefore, has that which is good become death to me? Let it not be! But the sin, that sin, might be manifest, was working death in me through what is good so that sin through the command might become an exceedingly great sinner. For we know that the Torah is Spiritual, but I am fleshly, sold under sin. For what I work I know not. For what I wish that I do not practice but what I hate, that I do. But if I do what I do not wish I agree with the Torah that it is good. And now, it is no longer I that work it, but the sin dwelling in me. For I know that in me, that is in my flesh, dwells no good. For to wish is present with me but to work the good I do not find. For the good that I wish to do I do not do, but the evil I do not wish to do, this I practice. And if I do that which I do not wish it is no longer I who work it, but the sin dwelling in me. I find therefore this law, that when I wish to do the good, that the evil is present with me. For I delight in the Torah of Elohim according to the inward man, but I see another law in my members, battling against the

Torah of my mind and bringing me into captivity to the law of sin which is in my members. Wretched man that I am! Who shall deliver me from this body of death? Thanks to Elohim, through Yeshua Messiah our Master! So then, with the mind I myself truly serve the Torah of Elohim, but with the flesh the law of sin." Rabbi Sha'ul, Romans 7:12-25

To break it down, Rabbi Sha'ul (Paul) is telling us that within the Torah is life and our instruction. Yeshua/Jesus is our Master of the Torah, through the spirit. We know that the Torah is the voice of God; we know that the Torah is His will, His perfect Will. In our minds, we know what to do, to say, and how to act. But, our flesh takes over. So often we have allowed the bad wolf, the dark dog, the evil creature to be fed. To win.

Are you a short-tempered person? Was your dad? Your mother? How about any of your children? Are they short tempered? These are soul traits, easy to recognize and they are fixable. It takes work, through discipline and The Torah and Yeshua/Jesus.

Ben Zoma asked, "Who is strong?" His answer: "Whoever controls their evil inclination." The *yetzer ha'ra*.

Your *yetzer ha'ra* will push you to do things you shouldn't and keep you from doing things you should. Again, Rabbi Sha'ul referred to it as 'the flesh'.

It will be tempting as bait. A little bit of this, a little bit of that, until you have lost your temper and now are screaming at your children. A little milk spilled. A tire goes flat, the keys are lost, the phone rings, a check bounces, a child hits another child, the dinner burns, the cup breaks, the computer freezes. You snap!

In *Everyday Holiness, The Path of Mussar*, Alan Morinis writes about Rabbi Yosef Yozel Hurwitz of Novarodok who shows the way the *yetzer ha'ra* works by exploiting what he calls a righteous opening. His example is Cain, who ultimately killed his brother, Abel. His first step toward that terrible act came with his reaction to God's acceptance of Abel's sacrifice but not his. Cain wanted his sacrifice to be accepted, too, which Rabbi Yosef Yozel Hurwitz calls a positive and righteous kind of jealousy. But it was still jealousy, all the same, and that is what created an opening for the *yetzer ha'ra*. He was led along until he committed the first recorded killing. [1]

We all have uniqueness and we all have transgressions, and there is a difference between the two. We also have those perfect gifts from above. Someone has the gift of giving, yet others reach into their pocket to give and change their mind. It is possible that you realize you should have more patience with your children, but then as soon as you resolve to be more patient, something happens to remind you that their slowness is making you late.

We can't change our character traits. But The Messiah can! We can do all things through The Messiah Yeshua! He will guide, comfort and help us as we learn to control them, to nurture them, and guide them until eventually they (those nasty soul traits that we don't like) are subdued or not even there. We can live with them, acknowledge them, and not allow them to take over our lives – through the Messiah. Once an alcoholic always an alcoholic, yet it is by choice whether you take that next drink or not. Remember, God did give us free choice in our lives! You can control it, and thousands do; and thus change the habits. You can change your habits which changes our future. And as Rabbi Messer teaches, your future is decided by your habits. Do you smoke cigarettes? It's not a sin to smoke cigarettes; however, your future could include lung cancer in your sixties. Not a very pretty picture, but a fact of 'habits'.

A twentieth-century Mussar master, Rabbi Eliyahu Lopian, explains the very being of our souls and Mussar. He defined Mussar as, "making the heart feel what the intellect understands." He continues, "Even when the intellect sees and understands, the heart, the seat of emotions, remains distant and cold."[2]

I'm praying for you right now. I don't know who you are, but I am asking The Father to give you grace and mercy and guidance as you work on your character traits and your habits. You are a set apart people, a child of The Most High; you are grafted in to the tree Israel (Romans 11) and Yeshua/Jesus is The Root. How strong is that! You are His Creation.

That last sentence is so important to grasp. *You are His creation.* Avoid being scornful with yourself. *The Ethics of the Fathers* teach that it is a powerful weapon of the Evil Inclination that convinces someone that he is spiritually worthless, because if that is so, then there is no reason for the person to try and better himself. Do not fall prey to that debilitating strategy! Every person can grow spiritually. When you pray, do not view yourself as a worthless person. It is your prayers and praise that The Father so anxiously awaits!

Rabbi Shapiro of Phoenix draws a parallel of a person as a caretaker. We are not the master of the garden but only the caretaker. Our garden, our inner home, the Temple of the Living God is housed with the *Ruach HaKodesh*, the Holy Spirit. We are neither the owner nor the Master.

But when we come to the ill fated conclusion that we are the master and that we own the residence, and our agenda is the agenda, then the temple gets turned, as in the Temple Days of Ancients, the cherubim turned away from one another.

To win the battle within, we must turn our attention towards the source, the master, YHWH. *"God, open Your hand and satisfy all living with Your will."* Psalms *Tehillim* 145:16

The Chafetz Chaim translates living here as *tzadek*, or righteous. And we are made righteous through the Master Yeshua Messiah. If we look at the source, if we go to the Master, we will become like the Master.

Our quest or answer here is not about fault or blame. If we place blame upon ourselves, or upon anyone else, we have redirected the message to something external instead of internal. Suffering is there to redirect our attention inward [3], to the *Ruach HaKodesh* which will in turn direct our paths to The Master.

The Ba'al Shem Tov, the master of the Chasidic movement was constantly correcting himself as a good character would. He was always checking his vision. Is it of the Master, or is it of myself.

Remember the Master desires to hear from the caretaker. He desires our prayers, our psalms, our petitions, and our love. Yeshua eagerly awaits to conquer the struggle, the battle within.

1. Everyday Holiness, The Path of Mussar, Alan Morinis
2. Everyday Holiness, The Path of Mussar, Alan Morinis
3. Rabbi Shapiro, Scottsdale Institute for Torah Studies, AZ

Make the days count instead of just counting the days

The Dream

I was a goat and I was tired of the same pasture. I was hot and the pond looked so wonderful. I jumped in and immediately sank. I was drowning and yet suddenly became able to breathe, though with difficulty; in the water. Over time, I was able to leave the bottom of the pond, where I had been sinking in the mud, and move around. Over time I was able to swim a little here a little there and my breathing became easier. Over time I was able to eat the minnows and plant life that grew in the pond. The pond was sustaining me. Over time I began to adapt.

Over time, my hair fell out and my raw skin became weak flesh. Over time, I began to sink once again in the mud. Breathing became difficult, until each breath through the water was almost impossible. I knew I was dying. I could no longer adapt. As hard as it was, I made it to the embankment and forced my hooves to climb, climb. Soon, after much work I was out of the pond. My skin was raw and exposed to the elements and breathing was strange. My hooves were weak and pliable.

Over time my hooves strengthened, my breathing became normal and my hair grew back. Over time I was once again able to graze in the pasture that I left. I was what I was meant to be and I was living.

Weird dream? Yes it is and I asked God to show me what it meant. He was showing me that we can adapt, but soon would die a spiritual death. If we live as He has not ordained, as we choose our own walk, we die spiritually. We are to live as *He* has ordained, as He has chosen. That means as hard as it is: to give it up, all to God.

(Why a goat? I don't know, but we raise them, and they are so stubborn that it probably was just reminding me of me....)

"*You have destroyed yourself O, Yisrael, but your help is in Me.*" Hosea *Hoshea* 13:9. Our help is in Him!

What we do exactly is consequences to, of and because of ourselves. They are our actions and reactions to other's actions. We can choose on which path and which manner we will act.

"*Take words with you, and return to YHWH. Say to Him, "Take away all crookedness, and accept what is good, and we render the bulls of our lips."*" Hosea *Hoshea*, 14:2.

The bulls that Hosea is referring to are the offerings of our mouths. What kind of offering will we render to The Lord? The bulls of our lips are the offerings of praise that we can render to The Lord for everything. Literally, everything! Who are we to complain or whine? He knows our sorrows, and our discomforts. He knows it all. When I was diagnosed with cancer God was not confused about that and thinking, 'Wow, where did *that* come from?'

The words that Hosea is referring to are the Words of the Torah. Not to literally take a Bible around with you and beat people over the head with it or yourself for that matter. But to take the Words of The Torah, The Life, The Name into our life, our being, or walk. To become what the Words say to become. To be the habit of God.

Rabbi Messer teaches that the Glory of God is us. The Glory of God is His Presence. We can *see* His glory in the earth, the animals, the seas, the trees, and the stars of the skies. The Glory of The Torah is *within* us. We are His created Glory, His manifestation is within us. Rabbi Messer asks a paradoxical question, do the fish have to learn to swim? Does a cow have to learn the moo? It, the Glory of God is already in them. And how much more for a person, who is created in the likeness of The Father? How much more Glory! [1] The Torah, His Word is already within us, we were created with it. We just have to acknowledge it and let it shine.

In the chapters in Genesis that contain the account of Jacobs ladder, our English Bibles stop at 'it': *"And he dreamed and saw a ladder set up on the earth, and its top reached to the heavens, and saw messengers of Elohim going up and coming down on it."* Genesis *Bereshith* 28:12.

The Hebrew actually reads: *"And he dreamed and saw a ladder set up on the earth, and its top reached to the heavens and saw messengers of Elohim going up and coming down on it with him."*[2]

Notice that the 'him' is not capitalized, meaning that Jacob saw himself ascending and descending upon the ladder with Yeshua.

"And He said to him, 'Truly, truly, I say to you, from now on you shall see the heaven opened, and the messengers of Elohim ascending and descending upon the Son of Adam." John, *Yohanan 1:51*.

The Messiah, Yeshua is the ladder. He with the heavenly hosts, are with us, we are always in a state of ascending and descending. Think of the old adage, 'two steps forward one step back'. Yeshua shows us this in one very important place in Scripture when He descends before He ascends. There is always a descent before there is an ascent. [3]

When we descend, we tend to think of is as trials, and in away that is true. Rabbi Sha'ul, Paul, tells us to count all trials as blessings. And that is so true, for with out our trials, we would not descend and then as in the laws of the universe, there would be no ascent.

We will never be in a constant state of ascending, for we are in this Earth, we are dealing with an animalistic nature. We have to think about our actions and reactions. There is a Hellenistic view that we should always be 'up', perfect, have a perfect life, children and so on. [4] Be happy get over it!

It's not that we don't desire that, it's that we try to achieve it with the wrong mindset. We can achieve Gods' shalom, but we must keep in check our attitudes and desires, needs and wants. Our character traits.

Our characters are shaped by certain events in our lives, and then we adapt to the way we are. "Oh, well, that's just me," is what we often tell ourselves, or our spouses. We get stuck in that space of time, in that state of being.

One of the teachings from Rabbi Messer of STBM, is about the six benefits of pain: [5]

1. It forces you to The Torah
2. You lean on God not men
3. Forces you to learn where you went astray
4. Forces you to long for His presence and healing
5. Pain forces you to listen for changes in God's instruction
6. It forces you to love whatever remains

Pastor Jay Howard of Simchat haMashiach, [6] taught on Amos 7:6, *"This is what He showed me, and see, YHWH stood on a wall made with a plumb line, with a plumb line in His hand, and YHWH said to me, 'Amos, what do you see?' And I said, 'A plumb line.' And YHWH said, 'See. I am setting a plumb line in the midst of My people Yisrael, no longer do I pardon them."*

Pastor Howard was a builder and a contractor for many years in Phoenix AZ, and he explained the precision of a plumb line. It is exact, unlike a level, which can read with error. How amazing that YHWH refers to Himself as a plumb line. We can never be a plumb line; we can never be that perfect ladder. But we can live our lives accordingly, and according to that plumb line and ladder; but only with The Messiah, Yeshua.

"...strengthening the beings of the taught ones, encouraging them to continue in the belief, and that through many pressures we have to enter the reign of Elohim." Acts 14:22

"Therefore, having been declared right by belief, we have peace with Elohim through our Master Yeshua Messiah, through whom also we have access by belief into this favour in which we stand, and we exult in the expectation of the esteem of Elohim. And not only this, but we also exult in pressures, knowing that pressure works endurance; and endurance, approveness, and approveness, expectation." Romans 5:1-5

"...not idle in duty, ardent in spirit, serving the Master; rejoicing in the expectancy, enduring under pressure, continuing steadfastly in prayer;..." Romans 12:11, 12.

"Great is my boldness of speech toward you; great is my boasting on your behalf. I have been filled with encouragement; I overflow with joy in all our pressure." 2Corinthians 7:4

We will have miserable days, that's a given. We will feel like dirt sometimes. We will be so angry with our spouses we could and some do, scream. We will wish we were somewhere else, somewhere warmer, nicer, and prettier. We will be annoyed with the driver ahead of us, behind us or next to us. We will have down days and down seasons in our lives.

But it is how we react to these days and times and seasons. We must not adapt to the out-sidedness of God's Will, of His living Word, or we die. Whether it's physically, financially, spiritually or emotionally, eventually we will die.

"Brothers, I do not count myself to have laid hold of it yet, but only this: forgetting what is behind and reaching out for what is ahead, I press on toward the goal for the prize of the high calling of Elohim Messiah Yeshua. As many then are perfect should have this mind. And if you think differently in any respect, Elohim shall also reveal this to you. But to what we have already attained, walk by the same rule, and be of the same mind. Become joint imitators of me, brothers, and observe those who so walk as you have us for a pattern." Philippians 3:13-17

"For the rest then brothers, we beg you and call upon you in the Master Yeshua that as you received from us how you should walk, and to please Elohim, you should excel still more." 1Thessalonians 4:1

The Torah is within us.

So:

Make everyone and everything a challenge in your life, a challenge to succeed in and for The Glory of God. [7]

1. Rabbi Ralph Messer, Simchat Torah Beit Midrash, Denver CO
2. Lexham Hebrew-English Interlinear Bible
3. Rabbi Ralph Messer, Simchat Torah Beit Midrash, Denver, CO
4. Pastor Jay Howard, Simchat haMashiach Beit Emunah, Bayfield CO
5. Rabbi Ralph Messer, Simchat Torah Beit Midrash, Denver, CO
6. Pastor Jay Howard, Simchat haMashiach Beit Emunah, Bayfield, CO
7. Pastor Jay Howard, Simchat haMashiach Beit Emunah, Bayfield, CO

If you have a hill to climb, waiting won't make it smaller

Putting it into Practice

The American culture is too busy. The Mussar Masters were not from this era; times were different. A lot different. Life as we know it now is high speed, fast. We never turn our cell phones off, even in a place where we are supposed to have them off, we put them on vibrate. We make sure we check into hotels with internet, our children have little white ear phones sticking out of their ears connected to the latest contraption that lets them view thousands of movies, songs, texts, and life. We spend hours searching cyberspace for something, anything, and our children spend an equal amount of time changing their private space on one of those spaces.

If you go to a gym, or if you walk, run, swim, lift weights, whatever you do to keep in shape, you allow yourself time. Maybe 30 minutes, maybe an hour, but you allow yourself time. So it must be with Mussar. You have to allow yourself time. You're going to have to make a few changes, get up a little bit earlier. Take a quiet lunch or go to bed just a little bit late. Don't watch that TV program and don't make that unnecessary phone call. Discipline: you can do it! Just allow yourself a little bit of time, somehow, somewhere.

"You can only get a feeling for your internal life when you are alone. With a half hour of being alone, you can come to feel things you never knew about yourself and see what you are lacking in spirituality. You will set new goals to reach. This can only be done if you spend time alone in seclusion for a half hour or so. In this way you can start to build your internal, spiritual world." Rabbi Shlomo Wolbe.

There are six basic steps to practicing Mussar. I added the seventh one and the eighth one listed had also been previously added.

1. Prayer and meditation
2. Silence
3. Diary Work
4. Chanting/Singing/Speaking
5. Contemplating actions and reactions
6. Visualizing
7. Fasting
8. Bearing another's burdens

Prayer. Our life without prayer is uncertain. Make prayer apart of your life. Ask God to grant you wisdom and guidance to reveal what He wants you to see. Most of all Praise His Holy Name. Whatever you do, whatever happens, praise Him. Some people like to ask of Him, demand of Him and want blessings from Him. And there is nothing wrong with that, but turn it around, Bless *His* Holy Name. "*Rejoice always, pray without ceasing...*" 1Thessalonians 5:16, 17

Reb Eliyahu Lopian, who spread Torah and inspired students in London, Jerusalem and Kelm, put together *A Collection of Talks*. In this paper, he mentions what R. Hona said, that whoever prays in the same place regularly invokes the help of the God of Abraham.

"*And Abraham arose early in the morning and went to the place where he had stood before The Lord.*" Genesis *Bereshith* 19:27.

"*And I will appoint a place for my people Israel and will plant them and they shall dwell in a place of their own and no longer be afraid, neither shall the children of wickedness oppress them again, as at the first.*" 2Samuel *2Shemu'el* 7:10. It is important to select a specific place for some of your prayers.

If you hop from place to place to pray, your mind becomes fragmented. For you to pray regularly at the same place and time, you will notice peace and to help your thoughts from wavering from one to another.

If you are a pet owner, do you feed your pet in the same location? Do you feed your dog by the washer one night and by the garbage the other, then outside, inside, up the stairs, down in the basement or in the bathroom the next night? Probably not. You might even have a regular bowl for his chow and a regular water dish. Maybe you even have a special mat that the dog eats on.

Our prayers to YHWH are our spiritual food. If we get in the habit of praying each morning in the same place, it will become *habit*. And what a fantastic habit!

Begin your prayer with "Blessed are You O God" (Elohim, Lord, HaShem, YHWH) but begin with praising Him. Your words are important, for they release the hidden corners of the heart. In words you will discover what is beneath them. Only then will you be able to get beyond the words and advance past those words and be in a state of sublime silence toward the All Mighty Father.

"*And in the same way the Spirit does help in our weakness. For we do not know what we should pray, but the Spirit Himself pleads our case for us with groanings unutterable.*" Romans 8:26

Change Your Life

Try it, first thing in the morning, even standing by your bed. Go into your closet, in your front room looking out at the beauty of His Creation or under your Tallit. But be consistent and you'll notice a change…in you.

"And Daniel when he knew that the writing was signed, went home and in his upper room with his windows open toward Jerusalem, he knelt down on his knees three times a day and prayed and gave thanks before his God, as he had done before." Daniel 6:10.

"And Yitshaq (Isaac) went out to meditate in the field in the evening." Genesis *Bereshith* 24:63.

Silence. We touched on that earlier. You'll need silence. Silence to hear Him, to hear yourself and silence to understand. You need silence to hear the Whisper that is of God. *"….a time to tear, and a time to sew; a time to be silent and a time to speak;…"* Ecclesiastes *Qoheleth* 3:7

But, there is a difference between silence, in listening to God and to speaking to Him. When you speak "I love you" to some one, it takes on a thousand more times of direct meaning than when you look at the person and 'think' it. Learn to be silent to hear Him and to let the Spirit take over your prayer.

"Hush all flesh, before The Lord, for He has roused Himself out of His set apart dwelling!" Zechariah *Zekaryah* 2:13 *"Tremble and do not sin, speak within your heart on your bed and be still. Selah."* Psalms *Tehillim* 4:4. Sit, breathe, pray and *shema*.

Diary work. This practice is time consuming at best, and an annoyance that most Americans don't have time for. Yet it is a very important part of Mussar. Keeping track of actions and reactions during the day and keeping track of what triggers your habits will be very important. Greater detail about diary work is mentioned later on in the book.

Chanting. This is nothing to be scared about. So many people will get buggy booed and superstitious about this word. Just repeat what you know! Sing Praises to God, sing to yourself and sing aloud. Have you ever heard a cantor? It is beautiful music. Make your own music to God. In Hebrew, it is called *gerushin* from *l'garish*, meaning to separate. By repeating the name of God over and over again you separate yourself from the drama that is swirling around and over you. [1]

Repeat words that heal and that offer life. Chanting comes with each phase and each character trait that you will be working on. For example, if you are working on patience, and your child spills milk all over you just as you are to leave, you can either yell at him or say maybe these words: Walk in God's ways…Walk in God's ways…Walk in God's ways… (Hebrew:

L'lechet darcho). So speak Life! *"Sing to Him a new song."* Psalms *Tehillim* 33:3

Contemplation. This takes practice. Too often we spout off with our emotions before we contemplate the whole scene. If I say this…, then what are the consequences? If I do that…, then what are those consequences? Contemplating our actions and reactions takes training. It's easier to fly off the handle, or let fear grip you and *then* contemplate. The practice needs to be done *before* our reaction to an action happens. There is a 20 minute rule in dieting. Wait 20 minutes after your smaller portions, and you will see that you are full. It takes those 20 minutes for our bodies to register 'full'. Wait a few seconds, a few minutes before speaking. Contemplating our actions and visualizing them, really go hand in hand. *"Consider the path of your feet, and all your ways are established."* Proverbs *Mishle* 4:26

There is another very important part of contemplation: why and where. Once you realize why and where a certain character trait may possibly come from, it is easier to deal with. "Oh, boy, my dad/mom had a short temper, his/her parent had a short temper, that's where I get it, and so that is where my son/daughter is getting it." Then you can take this into recognition, be aware of it and deal with it. It's not so scary and out of reach. It's correctable.

Who is wise? One who foresees the future consequences of his acts. Babylonian Talmud *Tamid* 32a

Visualization. Having vivid imagery will allow you the power of imagination.

"Strong mental impressions leave a trace that influences one's inner qualities, emotions, perceptions, judgments and behaviors. The intellect is not the most profound of the aspects of soul – it is not the root – but impressions (wholesome and unwholesome) gathered in the mind do pass down to the root and color and shape the soul-traits."[2] *"After these events, the word of The Lord came to Abram in a vision, saying, 'Do not be afraid, Abram. I am your shield; your reward is exceedingly great.'"* Genesis *Bereshith* 15:1

Fasting I've added fasting to the original list. Fasting in our Western culture is seriously lacking. In the eastern cultures, fasting is a way of life. Remember, the Bible is an eastern book. We have 'westernized' it. Many people in the western civilizations do fast, but most fasts are for physical cleansings and health reasons. I would like to encourage you to fast for your 'spiritual' health.

Yom Kippur is the Holiest Fast day. Israelites fast all over the world to get closer to The Father and to take a repentive look at themselves.

But day-to-day living is not *Yom Kippur*. It is day-to-day living with hectic schedules, problems, phone calls and just life. So, skip one meal. If you work in the job force, skip lunch and spend that time reading Scripture or praying. If you are a stay a home parent, skip breakfast or lunch and just sit and reflect on The Father. No matter if you have busy little ones, they are His Glory, too. And quite His Glory! Read a passage of the Bible to them. Lay on the floor while they eat their noodles & cheese and carrot sticks and stare up at the ceiling praising The Father. It works, and you can do it!

Fasting is a great part of our spiritual health. Fasting is cleansing ourselves for that brief moment in space and just relishing on Him and His Word.

"But I, when they were sick,
I put on sackcloth;
I humbled my being with fastings;
And my prayer would return to my own bosom."
Psalm, *Tehillim* 35:13

"So I set my face toward YHWH the Elohim to seek by prayer and supplications, with fasting and sackcloth and ashes." Daniel 9:3

"…and she was a widow of about eighty four years, who did not leave the Set Apart Place, but served Elohim with fastings and prayers night and day." Luke 2:37

"Then having fasted and prayed and having laid hands on them, they sent them away." Acts 13:3

"Do not deprive one another except with agreement for a time, to give yourselves to fasting and prayer. And come together again so that Satan does not try you because of your lack of self-control." 1Corinthians 7:5

This last verse is so applicable in what we are trying to obtain through our walk and Mussar. Don't let haSatan, the evil inclination try us. Keep your self-control! This verse does not state that haSatan, the evil inclination will come at us with a pointy red pitch fork. It is our self-control that he devices us to lose. It will be our own doings. Be aware, and steadfast in prayer, and in fasting.

There is a great story involving fasting. There was a holy man who desired to afflict his being with fasting. He made a vow that he would not eat from his own hand, but by the hand of others. He would only consume what others desired to bring him.

Days, turned into a couple of weeks and still this man had not eaten. No one brought him food! They came asking for blessings or brought other gifts – but no food! He was starving!

One day he went down to the river and prayed. A hand, just a hand came out of the water with a bowl. When the bowl reached the man, it was full of fish…and it kept replenishing itself, again and again. News traveled and people came from all over to see the bowl, touch the bowl, and worship the bowl. He became very irritated for no one wanted to hear about the source of the bowl. He asked his teacher, what he should do. The answer was to through the bowl back into the river. The man did, and the people stopped coming.

Sometimes we want to see the bowl and not the source. If you fast, keep your eyes on Yeshua the source and He will replenish your bowl. (Matthew 14 & Mark 6).

One other practice in Mussar is perhaps the greatest. That is bearing the burden of one another, of others. That's Yeshua!

Most of our habits circle around us. Do you suffer from fear? What is that fear centered on? Could it be that something will happen to you? Fear of the unknown for ourselves. Are you an impatient person? Why, because someone or something is keeping you from a feeling, a place, a certain time?

"And God created the man in His image, in the image of God He created him – male and female He created them." Genesis, Bereshith 1:27.

"Bear one another's burdens, and so complete the Torah of Messiah. For if anyone thinks himself to be somebody when he is not, he deceives himself." Galatians 6:2.

In his book, *Everyday Holiness, The Path of Mussar*, Alan Morinis writes that he has even heard of holiness meaning the absence of self interest.[3] He goes on to say that in helping others we encounter our own personal spiritual curriculum which provides us with an ideal opportunity to grapple with our own soul traits and grow spiritually.

The Alter of Kelm tells us that bearing the burden of others means acts of generosity, loving – kindness, compassion and care undertaking for the benefit of another.

Mussar is a way towards spiritual self-development. You are working on yourself, your traits and habits but not for the sole sake of yourself. By dealing with the issues of our heart and correcting habits that need correcting, thus nourishing our souls, we become the light that we are to be.

Change Your Life

We cannot see light; we see the reflection of the light. So, too, as we should be, the reflection of The Father's Love and His Divine Word. Mussar is not self-help, but rather a guide to correcting where we have become 'bent'. It is to help one make their path straight.

While flipping through the Christian channels on the television, I briefly heard a Christian lecturer teaching on anger. She was giving examples of being angry and asked the audience exactly what did Jesus have to say about it? She spoke loudly and aggressively to the audience, complete with anger scrunches between the eyebrows and she said, "So what did Jesus say to do? He said, 'DON'T!'"

Well, that's true. But how do I *don't*? Most of us realize the way we should behave. I would be amazed to hear someone say that Yeshua/Jesus said to pout, yell or gossip about someone.

I have to put into examination my whole life. Why am I this way?

I know that I should *don't*, you know you should *don't* but I/we need to get to that place where we *don't*. That is where the practice of Mussar, and most important, The Holy Spirit will take you.

The Chafetz Chaim was asked how he had such an impact on the Jewish world in the twentieth century, he answered that he set out to change the world and failed at that. He then set out to change the community of Poland but failed at that. Next, he set out to change the community of his hometown of Radin and still failed at that. He then set out to change his own family and failed at that as well. Finally, he decided to change himself and that is how he impacted the Jewish world.

We cannot control others, yet we try. We cannot change others, yet we try and will fail miserable. We cannot control our own selves, yet we impose our beliefs, feelings, opinions and desires upon others.

Rabbi Rami Shapiro in his book, *The Sacred Art of Lovingkindness, Preparing to Practice* , tells us that we can not really even change ourselves unless and until we encounter reality. When we really see how we act or react to a situation, then we can change that. And how what we do impacts our family, the people and the world around us. [4]

To forgive.

I cannot do anything about a family member who is unforgiving. But *I* can forgive. I can change me by changing the way I react to others and life around me.

Wisdom in The Lord will give us the *Yirah* to move ahead. Then the wisdom we gain can be moved into action.

'The mitzvah of tefillin is symbolic of this precept. One places the tefillin on the hand first and then on the head, and when he removes them, the tefillin of the hand remain on until those of the head are taken off. Thus the head tefillin, representing wisdom are never worn without the hand tefillin, representing action. Ideas and wisdom are only valuable if they are translated into action.'[5]

1. The Sacred Art of Lovingkindness, Preparing to Practice, Rabbi Rami Shapiro
2. Everyday Holiness The Path of Mussar, Alan Morinis
3. Everyday Holiness The Path of Mussar, Alan Morinis
4. The Sacred Art of Lovingkindness Preparing to Practice, Rabbi Rami Shapiro
5. Pirkei Avos, The Ethics of The Fathers, Mesorah Publications

Remember that strength is gained by meeting resistance

Review

Yirah, the fear and awe of God. *Pirkei Avos, Ethics of The Fathers,* tells us that in the service of God there are three levels. The lowest is the fear of retribution, where man is basically concerned with his own self-preservation. On a higher level is the love of God, where we cannot do enough for Him. And the most elevated form of the relationship is the fear/awe; *the yirah,* due to God's exaltedness. (Rambam)

- Emotions. Our emotions are tied in with our character traits. Our character traits come from our issues of the heart. Our character traits can also come from our DNA. There is a difference between emotion and intelligence.
- Communication. How we communicate in either verbal or non-verbal ways greatly affects the person we are sending the message to. How we communicate also will be manifested by our character traits and emotional intelligence.
- Mussar. The word means correction, instruction and ethics. It is a way of life, and a path. It is a reconditioning of our soul traits, our emotions and character.
- The Purpose. Our purpose in life is to glorify God and to be a set apart people, and have joy in The Messiah. You already are a set apart people!
- Generational Curses. In Deuteronomy 27, 28 & 29 we are told and given complete instruction in regards to our life connecting with The Father.
- The Battle. There is a battle within us, the *yetzer ha'tov,* the good inclination and the *yetzer ha'ra,* the bad inclination.
- Putting it into practice. This is diligence and discipline. Prayer, silence, diary writing, chanting, contemplation, imagery and fasting are all part of the process. These conditions are very important parts of the Mussar.

I was slack on the diary writing, and was having difficulties processing information when I would flare up, or lose my patience. It was only through the writing of the events that I could see where I was having the most issues.

So, I stress to you, be conscientious in each step. Take your time. Listen to The Father as He guides you through this process. And be very honest with yourself. Is it always someone else's fault? Or is it how we react? Be careful and wise with evaluations and words you choose. Look for the little moment that made you snap, or doubt or fear. You'll find it, it's there. You are not a bad person, so don't beat yourself up: you are The Glory Of God.

Not that I have already received, or already been perfected, but I press on to lay hold of that for which Messiah Yeshua has also laid hold of me. I do not count myself to have laid hold of it yet, but only this: forgetting what is behind and reaching out for what lays ahead. Philippians 3:13

The Character Traits

"My brothers, count it all joy when you fall into various trials." James *Ya'aqob* 1:2

The Ways of The Tzaddikim list 28 soul traits, referring to each one as a gate.[1] The soul traits listed in the book *Cheshbon Ha-Nefesh* list thirteen character traits.[2]

Alan Morinis in his book, *Everyday Holiness The Path of Mussar*,[3] covers thirteen somewhat different soul traits than the two previous books.

In this book there are two sections of eight. The sixteen soul traits that are covered in the second half of this book are by no means an extensive list. Some you may find do not pertain to you, and others are your very breath. The reason why there are two separate listings of eight character traits in this book, is that the number eight has a Hebrew meaning of: 'new beginnings'. Yeshua was circumcised on the eighth day, we are told to circumcise our hearts, and that our hearts will be circumcised. When we work on ourselves, our emotions, our character, we do circumcise our hearts. We open the closed heart.

So, this is a 'new beginning' for you.

Below is a list of character traits that are prevalent in the human race. This by all means is not a complete list. Go through the list, finding your character traits and what you need to work on. After you complete the character traits that are listed in this book, you will understand how to work on others. Some that you may want to work on may not even be mentioned in the list below. But the process is the very same, and it won't be difficult for you to manage and work on, once you understand the idea of the progression through Mussar.

Character Traits:
- Anger
- Apathy
- Arrogance
- Awareness
- Calmness
- Caution

- Cleanliness
- Compassion
- Concentration
- Courage
- Cruelty
- Defiance
- Decisiveness
- Determination
- Diligence
- Discretion
- Empathy
- Envy
- Equanimity
- Fairness
- Faith
- Falsehood
- Fear
- Flattery
- Forgetfulness
- Forgiveness
- Frugality
- Generosity
- Gratitude
- Greed
- Hate
- Honesty
- Humility
- Integrity
- Jealousy
- Joy
- Laziness
- Love
- Loving-kindness
- Lying
- Mercy
- Modesty
- Obedience
- Openness
- Order

- Patience
- Pride
- Punctuality
- Regret
- Repentance
- Responsibility
- Remembrance
- Righteousness
- Separation
- Shame
- Shyness
- Silence
- Simplicity
- Sincerity
- Strength
- Trust
- Truth
- Willingness
- Worry
- Zeal

Remember, this is all about improvement, in truth looking at reality, looking at ourselves, our actions and reactions, changing and learning. We are here to shine the Glory of God made manifest in us and we are here to be that set apart people that He has already made us. That is the free gift of holiness. Also, in all things we must be aware of the influence we have on others. The effect we have on others will shape their behaviors and reactions, too. Our actions and reactions can become stumbling blocks, so we therefore take into our substance, the burdens of others.....to not be a stumbling block to another.

We can't help but have regret on the actions that do not glorify The Father, and specifically actions that hurt someone else, which do not by any means glorify The Father. Apologize, ask for forgiveness and begin again. But don't camp out there in that hurt. When you stay focused on your sins, you are in fact keeping attention on you. You are saying, "oh look at me, I am too wretched even for God, too awful to keep trying. So if I am too wicked for God, then I am too wicked to try and be kind to those that are wicked to me. I can't forgive or ask for forgiveness." And the cycle continues, and you stay in that season. Acknowledge, resist, and reverse.

When you stay focused on the hurt that was done to you, again, in reality you are staying focused on yourself, another act of self-importance. Forgive them and move on.

Keep your focus and keep moving forward, and make your course corrections.

Just as the Hebrew approach to life is exactly that: a lifestyle and is not something you 'believe' in, as in the Hellenistic mindset of 'What do you believe?' So, too, Mussar is not something you learn, it is something you do. It is an action. It is a verb.

Tikkun middot ha'nefesh means improving the traits of the soul. You are already filled with the Holy Spirit, the Light and Salt of the earth. You are already filled with the Glory of God, His Torah and Word. You are already on Jacobs' ladder and Yeshua is there with you. You just have to let go and view this whole principal as an improvement.

Jacob wrestled with The Lord, and asked His name. Remember that name again translates into 'walk'. The Lord changes Jacobs name to Israel, he is at that point elevated, at that point Jacob has had a status change. Jacobs' walk changed upon that soul improvement, that season of change. However, notice that through out the Scriptures, he is referred interchangeable to Jacob then Israel, then back to Jacob and Israel again. Where as Abraham' after the name status change from Abram to Abraham, is never again called Abram.

Jacob is up and down the ladder, descending and ascending.

Rabbi Israel Salanter, the great rabbinic sage, 1810-1883, was once spending the night at the home of a shoemaker. It was very late at night when the Rabbi observed the shoemaker still working by a candle, almost to the end of the flame.

Rabbi Salanter commented to the shoemaker of the lateness of the night, and that his candle was about to go out, yet still he worked.

The shoemaker responded with, "As long as the candle is burning, it is still possible to mend."[1]

Liken the candle to life, The Light of Life, and the light within us, which is The Messiah. As long as we have that gift of life, there is time to mend, to reconcile, to move forward and press ahead.

Everything that happens to man is part of a Divine plan; there is no such thing as coincidence or accident (commentary on Exodus 13:16)[2].

When we look at the world and decipher it as if it was created for us, then we can have the mindset of 'oh they did that, or, they caused that.' But when we look at the creation of God with the mindset that the world was created for all, we realize that we are not solely the center of God's story, and His Divine plan is for all. It takes great cultivation in our mindset to observe the events in the world as happening to a whole. It is necessary to realize that events that happen are the source of a Divine Will. But God will always show us what we need to see at that moment in time.[3]

1. Everyday Holiness The Path of Mussar, Alan Morinis
2. Pirkei Avos, The Ethics of the Fathers, Mesorah Publications
3. Rabbi Shapiro, Scottsdale Institute for Torah Studies, AZ

"Let your light so shine before men, so that they see your good works and praise your Father who is in the heavens." Matthew, Mattithyahu 5:16

LETTING GO AND CHANGING

MUSSAR IN PRACTICE

PART TWO

Beginning

Beginning.
    Many times in our lives we begin again. A fresh start, a new look, a new house, a new beginning. It can happen randomly with out pre-thought or planning, such as an untimely death of a spouse or a child. Whether we like it or not, whether we understand it or not, we begin again.

    A sudden illness can trigger a new start. After cancer treatment, I began again. A new hairstyle when my hair grew out, a new and different body; not one that I would have chosen; but a different body nonetheless. Most importantly, I gained a new outlook on life.

    When a teenager gets those braces off or gets that always craved for drivers' license; that is the beginning of a new life. Taking off those training wheels, learning to read, those too, are great milestones of our lives.

    Everyday is a new beginning. Everyday can be a fresh start.

"Baruch ata adonai, Eloheinu melech ha'olam, shehechiyanu, v'kiyamanu, v'higiyanu l'zman hazeh."

"Blessed are you O Lord our God, King of the universe who has kept us in life and sustained us and allowed us to reach this moment."

    I repeated that blessing every morning when I woke up. Woo-Hoo! I'm alive! It was really good to be alive. And it really *is* good to be alive, so I repeat it to this day. And, aren't you glad, so grateful to be alive?

    Let's create a new day for ourselves with our character traits. As you enter into these next 8 weeks you will be working on a specific character trait each week. Again, the list is not exhaustive at all, and if you need to work on a trait twice – go for it! As the weeks go by, you will be able to recognize in yourself what traits need to be addressed and then you will know how to continue the process with the last eight traits that are listed.

But at first, spend one week for each trait; that will give you 8 weeks of work. Then go month by month, reviewing and checking each day. After a year, go through the notes and the diary that you have written, and you will begin to eliminate the traits that you no longer need to work on, the soul traits that no longer plague you.

Every trait will need a code word, or a group of words that you will repeat as you work on that trait. For equanimity my code words were: rise above it…rise above it… I would repeat those words until I felt a calmness again come over me, and believe me, I repeated them often. In fact, I use them to this day as I feel myself beginning to get sucked into a bad emotional charge. It can happen very randomly, for instance riding in the car with my husband and I don't particularly like what he is saying. So, instead of jumping in and arguing, I repeat: rise above it…rise above it. For the outcome is to change myself, my reaction, not change him to fit my personality flukes at that precise moment.

Every morning of that particular week that you are working on that particular character trait, repeat the code word. Be sure and consider how it can be used that day. Consider what you have to do that day in your responsibilities to God and to man and make your priorities. Before you end the day, review the activities of the day and make notes of the situations that made you react in a certain way. It is only then that you will begin to really recognize a certain character trait and just exactly how it was manifested that day. And remember, every morning, you can choose your attitude for the day, it's up to you. It's a choice!

Let's say that you are working on patience, and that particular day you were able to 'keep' your patience all day. Very good! But make notes as to why you were able to keep your patience. The traffic was good, the dog didn't get loose, the phone worked, the computer didn't freeze, the baby kept sleeping, the boss was nice. Whatever it was, make a note.

You will begin to see a pattern. Is it little things that bother me? Or am I able to keep my patience until 'I snap'. Or, does patience only work for me when the environment around me is perfect to my comfort zone. Ah, ha, you will see a pattern.

For each trait there is a section for daily evaluation and weekly responses to see if you were able to work on that trait. Keep going, don't quit and day by day, week by week, season by season and year by year you will see character traits either change or disappear, and the results will be amazing.

It is taught; that whatever thoughts are hidden in the heart accompanies us at all times, and based on their strength, will affect us both consciously and unconsciously.

What this statement is alluding to, is that if a person is full of pride, he will walk and act accordingly, not even being aware that his head is held high, or that he wants to speak first, or even that she is aware of her dress and comparing her 'modesty' to that of others.

So, please, be very aware of your heart. Remember, this is a change you are after. And the change is really not a change at all, but us taking a good look at reality and taking a different path. Therefore, the word change in this sense is a misnomer, and then again it isn't. No offense, no pouting, no excuses. Be aware of each situation, and be willing to change, to redirect. Remember to look in the mirror and to point to the enemy! And don't get discouraged. Rabbi Messer teaches that we don't decide our future, we decide our habits and our habits decide our future. And motivation can fade, but habits won't. So be aware of the habits in your life. Are they spiritually killing you? Or are they uplifting you and others? Are your habits a reflection of The Messiah? Or are they some habits that you could afford to change? Discipline is necessary for any change. God desires obedience and delayed obedience is in actuality disobedience. (Rabbi Messer)

Eight Weeks

I have added a counter trait after each character trait. For instance, as you work on patience you are really working on impatience and eliminating that negative character trait. I think it's so important to replace negativity with positivism, therefore, when working on the character trait 'joy' we will be eliminating 'worry' as the drag–you-down negative trait. You can't have worry if you are full of His joy. This does not mean you have to have a Pollyanna outlook on life, or to see things through rose- colored glasses. You can be discerning and careful and wise, but you won't be filled with worry. And remember, it is His joy that we are to be full of. Not our own. His joy takes away our worry as His joy is ever present and ours fluctuates with day to day living.

We are working on our character traits, our very souls and as a root; character is defined by integrity, which gives us wholeness. These next eight positive traits bestow a personal integrity and wholeness, connected to The Father. So, as you gain perspective into your soul, you will arise to the situations that cause you impatience and you will begin to see a pattern.

In this book we will work on strengthening our positive traits, or gaining positive soul traits that we may not possess at this certain time.

To me, if I concentrate on a negative soul trait, such as fear, then I am concerned with fear. *Oh, don't fear, oh don't fear.* So, I am putting 'fear' into my blood. But if I concentrate on truth, the whole truth of a situation, and bring The Messiah, who is The Truth and His Word into my heart, my focus becomes Him. What a calming effect that truly is. The fear is replaced with the truth of the reality at that point of time and fear dissipates.

HaSatan would love for us to have ourselves fixed on our negative traits. We would feel so worthless, wouldn't we? That would initiate sort of a narcissistic attitude, then, focusing on our unworthiness and trying to bring The Father down. For if we condemn ourselves as the very Creation of The Father, we are in fact trying to bring Him down to a different level. When I write that the enemy is in the mirror, let's get that conquering attitude, that: hey, that impatience within me is the enemy; I'm going to conquer that!

I desire to change that habit of losing my temper so easily, and I desire to stop and listen and wait a few moments. I build my integrity and I change my habits, thus creating change in my future. If a habit is smoking, your future could include lung cancer. If a habit is yelling at people, your future could include no friends. Pretty grim.

The eight character traits and the counterparts:
1. Equanimity/anger
2. Patience/impatience
3. Joy/worry
4. Order/laziness
5. Truth/fear
6. Silence/arrogance
7. Humility/pride
8. Loving Kindness/bitterness

There are a few things to do before you work on each trait. First of all, breathe. We don't breathe deep enough in our culture. Dr. Andrew Weil encourages deep breathing in his articles and books. So, breathe deep. Feel the life in you. I know it sounds silly, but it makes one 'stop'. You have to be conscious about breathing deep. Not just breathing, but breathing deep.

Just think of the visits to the doctors' office. He has to tell us to 'breathe deep' or 'take a deep breath'. We don't just do it as an involuntary thought. In fact, most of the time we are breathing very shallow, especially if we do not 'rise above' things.

You will find yourself stopping, breathing, and considering things. Prayer just automatically follows. It's amazing! Stop, look out your window, breathe deep, and praise The Father. Are you alive? Has He allowed you another day to glorify Him? Amazing, isn't He?

'No preordained force in the universe, not even God, forces man to act the way he does (Rashi and Rav). Rambam and R'Yonah teach: 'and yet man is granted free choice.' God knows what man will do; this advanced knowledge in no way can affect the choice of man. Man enjoys total freedom of choice. The Torah teaches this adage of faith: [1] *"I have placed life and death before you, blessing and curse; and you shall choose life."* Deuteronomy *Debarim* 30:19.

In the 14th chapter of Hosea, we are told to take words with us. *"Take words with you and return to YHWH. Say to Him, "Take away all crookedness, and accept what is good, and we render the bulls of our lips."* Hoshea 14:2

"I shall heal their backsliding..." Hoshea 14:4

"I shall be like the dew to Yisra'el. He shall blossom like the lily and cast out his roots like Lebanon." Hoshea 14:5

Pastor Jay Howard taught on Hosea 14:2, explaining that in Hebrew the word for *words* was *Debarim*, or Deuteronomy. That doesn't mean to pack the book of Deuteronomy around, as we might think in a Western mindset. But rather, take His Words with us, His Torah, His teaching and instruction. We are to take His character traits found in the Torah, the 613 principles of God.

In verse four, we are told that He, God Almighty heals our backsliding. How does He do that? With grace only? No, through His Words, His teaching and instructions, His Torah, and through His grace, mercy and love. Unconditional love.

Verse five states that He is like the dew to Israel. Dew in Deuteronomy 32, *Debarim*, is Words. His teaching, His rain and His instruction, which falls on the righteous and unrighteous.

We can change, but remember He heals our backsliding. He is our dew. He is our rain. He is our teaching, our instruction. Use Him and the Scriptures. You will gain wisdom, which will gain honor and will glorify Him.

The Chapters

The next chapter starts with Equanimity with the counter trait of anger. It is very important to place this as the first character trait to work on, for 'to rise above it all' is the first step in a reality check, in the 'change' that we so desperately seek.

If anger is one of your weaknesses, as it was/sometimes is, mine, then the lesson of equanimity helps so much in that area. As you step in the puppy puddle when you arrive home, rise above…rise above! Do not lose your temper in that. Stop, breathe, okay, think how gross it is, how cold and wet your sock now is, and how yucky your foot feels, but really stop and contemplate. It's just puppy piddle, it's just a sock, it can be washed, and your foot can be rinsed. It's not worth raising your blood pressure, hardening your arteries and tightening your stomach. Rise above it!

'Tikkun middot ha'nefesh'- Improving the traits of the soul.

Dear Father, as we begin, let us glorify You in all things. Help us to shift our character traits to magnify Your Holy Name and be the light and salt that we are to be. In Yeshua's name, Amen and Amen..

1. Pirkei Avos, The Ethics of the Fathers, Mesorah Publications

You can't do much about your ancestors, but you can influence your descendants enormously. Anonymous

Equanimity

"Pursue peace with all and set apartness without which no one shall see The Master." Hebrews 12:14

Composure, calmness, level-headedness, equability, self-control and poise. Those are the words that my computer listed when I clicked the synonyms for equanimity. Let's think about those six words and what comes to mind.

When I think of composure I think of a subordinate being disciplined by a boss or higher ranking official and standing there listening. My son is a firefighter and he has explained to us that in the fire department, as in the police department and military there are ranks and certain procedures and protocol.

Calmness reminds me of my Dad when I came running to him after taking a very bad spill on my red bike. My knees and palms were pretty bloody and I had a cut lip, but he never let on to me that he was upset. He took me in his arms and helped me by soothing and calming me. He calmed me, he never yelled OMG! Call 911! (for those of you that are dated, like me, OMG means o my gosh...I learned that from my kids' texting....)

When I hear the words 'level-headed' I think of my husband, listening intently to our two boys after their fighting, as they try and explain away their behavior, and him not becoming angry.

Equability reminds me of taking tests in college. Being nervous but confident and focusing on the problems at hand. State the answers, not the problems.

Self-control is when you can smash your thumb with a hammer and you don't cuss!

When I hear the word poise, I think of a beautiful runway model that just wobbled on her high heel but smiles nonetheless and keeps going.

Aren't these great words? Wouldn't you love to have self- control, to be level-headed, and to be calm?

The Hebrew word for equanimity is *erech apayyim*, literally long faced. Think about your posture and facial expressions when you sit in deep prayer. Fasting will do that too, and Yeshua warns us to not look like we are fasting. Smile!

One of the most irritating situations to me is when I step in a puppy or dog puddle as I mentioned in the previous chapter. During the winter where I live, it gets pretty cold, so often when my family and I go out to a movie or dinner together, we have left the dogs in the house. We have five children, so it just makes perfect sense to have five dogs. Hmmm.

Upon coming home, the house is dark (we're on solar) and there you have it, a puddle that I step in.

Rise above it, rise above it. Calmness, composure.

Now, granted, that is a minor incident, and we have much more serious things to deal with, but it's a start.

The words that were listed at the beginning could be your code words, or: rise above it, or *menuchat ha nefesh*, calmness of the soul.

There is a difference between peace of mind and calmness of the soul. Peace is a tangible gift, one that our Messiah gives us, freely. But to accept that peace and to develop calmness of the soul is a learned event.

We are a wondering people, looking for peace of mind. 'Oh, if I only had peace!' Calmness of the soul, in any situation, gives us that peace, that tranquility. It is an elevation of ones' character where news becomes just news, neither good nor bad, but just news.

Upon the writing of this chapter, the nation and the world watched as the stock market plunged. Can hysteria or panic or anger at our government do anything about it? No, but if we realize the causes of our reactions, we can use that for a positive outcome. Whether we save money, cut up credit cards, don't invest in certain areas or change our political votes, we react towards a positive means instead of a panic reaction.

When I was diagnosed with cancer, I wanted to panic. I felt my heart begin to race, my mouth went dry and fingers tingled. It was the strangest sensation, sort of like being suffocated. The room was spinning and I felt as if I was either going to throw up or pass out. I stopped right there and prayed. I don't know what I said, I only remember that I reached out for help and received calmness, a little bit of that peace that I craved.

My husband contacted Rabbi and Maureen Messer and his advice to me was outstanding. He told me to keep my focus and beware of the counterfeits.[1]

To keep my focus was grounded advice. Okay, so this wasn't bad news, it was just news and now I have to deal with it. Quit wringing my hands and think and get focused, to rise above it. We had a lot of decisions to make, and advice was all over the place, (there is way too much fantastic and random information out there for someone single-handedly to digest).

The Father brings us tests, as we are the clay and He is the Potter. He does not tempt us, but we are always in tests and seasons. If our lives are not filled with tests and trials, we are probably dead. And nothing is brought to us by mistake. *Pirkei Avos* teaches that everything that happens to man is part of a Divine Plan; there is no such thing as accident or chance. Even when man is harmed by his fellow man, it is an expression of God's will.

When my son and I were leaving Phoenix to come back to Durango, we had a good opportunity to practice equanimity. My son happened to buy a small, about the size of my thumb, metal cap gun at the market. He packed that toy cap gun in the zipper compartment of his backpack. We went through the security check points, got all our belongings on and in order and left to go to the gate. While walking down the hallway, a TSA employee runs after us shouting something of a gun. Needless to say, it was pretty chaotic, for us and them. I was quite scolded and so was my son. Equanimity played a huge role that day in my life.

When one becomes angry with another person or takes revenge on him for a wrong, he is presumptuous to think that his fellow man had the independent capacity to harm him in the first place and does not take into account that of God's will. Otherwise, he would go to God as the source of his trials and would have no reason to be angry with the person who hurt him. Such anger is a form of idolatry for he assigns sovereign power to another human being when there is really no such thing. Therefore, it is taught to not anger easily, for it is a form of denial for all the events that occur in the world by The Source.

Anger is a fool, Proverbs 14:16. It stirs up strife, Proverbs 29:22. Anger affects our bodies, Proverbs 14:30, and an angry man is likened to a torrent, Proverbs 27:4.

When I was diagnosed, God wasn't putting His hand on His Head and saying, 'Wow, I didn't see that coming.' No, His presence is before me. Remember the Israelites in the wilderness, the cloud and the fire was before them, not dragging after them, sulking and worrying. So sing to yourself the words of a Paul Wilbur's song, *"In Your Presence, that's where I belong..."* You are in His Presence!

How can I learn to rise above anything if I have nothing to rise above? These tests that we are given lets us give rise to the life that we are given.

If I am satisfied with my spiritual walk, I will rot where I am. Take each test, rise above it, and keep moving forward.

We are to be the salt of the earth and salt has a definite flavor, a little bite to it. If we have experienced nothing, then we are salt less. How can I help someone with grief or anger or impatience if I've never been there? Yet I am to move forward. If I am given a test, and I do not rise above it, I will be given the same test again only to remain in that season of life until I rise above and conquer and learn from the test.

Mussar teaches tell us to rise above things both good and bad. That is parallel to the Scripture says that it is easy to love the lovable, yet hard to love the unlovable.

If some one waves me on in traffic, I usually speak 'thank you' and move my car ahead. If some one cuts me off, what could/would be my reaction? Possibly anger, impatience, and a louder voice than the previous example. But if I look at each situation as just that, a situation, I can rise above both. What the first driver did was his/her choice and what the second driver did was his/her choice. I have no control over their actions. But I do have control over my reaction.

With the presence of God moving before us, and the power of the Holy Spirit, we have the ability to take dominion over a situation as we are told in Genesis. It is not by might but by the Spirit of God that we win the battles. We are not to be afraid, but we are to be strong.

When a situation arises, take dominion over it, instead of 'it' taking dominion over you. If you are in a working situation and there is unnecessary confrontation, take dominion over it, rise above it. Ask The Father to give you the strength to get beyond it and to see what He would desire that you see. If nothing else, stop and pray. Breathe. Acknowledge, resist, and reverse.

A wonderful Godly women that was instrumental in my early years as a new Christian died after I had known her just three years. At Kit's funeral her son told a remarkable story about her.

They were in a store together, to return an item. It was crowded, and busy. The sales clerk was very impatient and snapped at Kit, repeatedly. When Kit and her son left the store, he was upset and complaining but all she said was, 'well, that was interesting.'

What a way to look at life!

Anger can be a justifiable emotion. But it's a trait that we need to have little of and keep in check. For anger can easily turn into rage. Yeshua was angry with the sellers in the Temple, but He had a mission, to move them out. To be rid of them. Jesus is also perfect and we're struggling to become those set apart people that we can be. Somehow, don't you just know that Yeshua was not going to choke one of those sellers or whip an animal? No, He *freed* the animals, turning over cages and turning over the money, bringing the coins to the *ground, the dust*. Very purposeful was His example. His anger was in check, a righteous anger.

Rabbi Eliezer in *Pirkei Avos, Ethics of the Fathers* tells us that it is really impossible never to get angry, so the *mishna* teaches to not anger *easily*.

Rabbi Eliezer explains a very key point to the consequence of anger. We are to let our fellows' honor be as dear to us as our own, and do not anger easily. By controlling our anger, we are sure to not diminish our fellow mans' honor. A person lost in a rage of anger is bound to debase his fellow man; therefore the second part is a means for achieving the first.[2]

When we read about a little child being abused, or believers in The Lord being tortured, we become righteously angry. Angry at the situation! Soon, our anger turns to a positive trait though, as we rise above it and do something with our feelings. To do something positive with those emotions is God helping us to rise above just sitting in our chairs watching the news and becoming angry at the scene on the TV. Get up, and serve that situation.

Unrighteous anger becomes self-centeredness when we allow ourselves to become angry or enraged at any situation that bothers *us*. At that point I am solely focused on myself. 'Oh, her behavior…their driving…their whining…makes me so mad…' And again, I am usually thinking or saying ugly thoughts or statements about my fellow man, and therefore degrading his honor.

Often, becoming angry causes us to make rash statements and it blocks our ability to communicate compassionately. What others may say or do can be the stimulus but never the cause of our feelings. We can see that our feelings result from how we choose to act or react in any given situation. When we focus on the wrongs of others, instead of our reactions, we are out of touch with the reality of the situation. We are so used to blaming other people and becoming angry with them when we feel our needs aren't being met, hence we can't get to the issue, Proverbs 14:17.

In the book *Non Violent Communication* by Marshall Rosenberg he gives an example of dealing with irritation that could soon turn to anger, if left to fester as the original feeling.

"Their cancellation of the contract really irritated me." This irritation can lead to anger. Instead, Marshall Rosenberg gives the better example:

"When they cancelled the contract I felt really irritated because.....".[3] Whatever the reason, the receiver of the message was not finding fault with the company that cancelled the contract. He was acknowledging what was causing his irritation and learned to identify that cause instead of pointing and blaming.

If one explodes in anger, he has at that moment in time lost the ability to pray. It is crucial, therefore, before the explosion to stop even for a mille second and pray. Breathe, pray, breathe, pray.

The advice from *Pirkei Avos* in regards to man and his free will really made me think. At first, I was in disagreement with that statement, as we are all given free will, so the person in the car ahead of me had/has the free will/choice to cut me off, or slow me down, or flip me off. But really?

But it comes to reason, that the explanation from *Pirkei Avos* is in fact very true. Just relate to the example of YHWH hardening Pharaohs heart, again and again. This is the irony that is so hard for our human minds to grasp. God is in ultimate control, yet we all have free will. When I accept reality with compassion, it allows me to employ it with equanimity and to move on.

When I find myself angry with an individual, maybe it would behoove me to consider everything and certainly ask The Father what He is trying to show me, instead of blaming the other person and becoming angry and vengeful at their anger or at the hurt that I may feel.

Rabbi Shapiro teaches that the sixth attribute of loving kindness is equanimity. 'Nothing is ever ideal; it is just the way it is. Realizing this is at the heart of what it is to develop equanimity.' [4]

Equanimity, rise above, calmness of the soul. Breathe, stop, pray, visualize and acceptance.

Keep your focus, keep moving forward, take dominion and rise above it.

---

1. Rabbi Ralph Messer, Simchat Torah Beit Midrash, Denver, CO
2. Pirkei Avos Ethics of The Fathers, Mesorah Publications, ltd.
3. Non Violent Communication, A Language of Life, Marshall B. Rosenberg Ph.D.
4. The Sacred Art of Lovingkindness Preparing to Practice, Rabbi Rami Shapiro

Change Your Life

<u>*Notes*</u>   <u>*Week One*</u>   <u>*Equanimity*</u>

Code word or words:

Situations to recognize:

Equanimity:

Day One

Day Two

Day Three

Day Four

Day Five

Day Six

Day Seven

The Exercise:

Equanimity and anger. Two opposite sides of the scale. To work with these character traits we have to create situations that will cause us to get angry and then will give us the opportunity to rise above it. Equanimity is not limited to anger, however. Insults and flattery are two major components that will rub our very ego to its core. Each confrontation will dive us into pride and arrogance or injury.

Here are a couple of exercises that you may try, though they are not extensive at all and merely suggestions.

Drive at the most congested part of the day, say five o'clock rush hour. Take wrong turns causing yourself to get further away from your destination – home. Be aware of your blood pressure as you sit in the traffic. Be very aware of the motorist that won't let you cut in, and be very aware when *you* allow someone cut in ahead of you.

Go to the bank or the market at the busiest part of the day. Compliment the teller or the checker. Compliment someone at church/synagogue that has never approached you, and be very aware if your flesh desires a compliment back. Are you being nice for a reason? What is your motive? We are kind because each is a Holy Soul.

Rise above all things.

For anger, you will need to create a situation that you would normally lose your temper.

My situation was breaking something that was full of a liquid, like milk or ketchup or sticky juice, just as I was about to start a project. So, whatever your project is, painting a room, watching a movie, working on the computer, reading to your child, bathing the dog, whatever it may be, pick one, and get set up for it. Be involved in it, truly involved with your project. Then leave the project, find a container, fill it up with a liquid and then drop it. Then you will have a mess that demands your attention and you must abandon your project – for a time. But, you'll discover that it really isn't that bad! Just clean up the mess – life goes on.

Maybe you have a longer temper. A good exercise is to find a website that you totally disagree with, one that causes the flesh to rise up in you. Are you an environmentalist? Then go to a hunting site. Are you pro life? Go to a pro-choice site. Are you a democrat? Go to a republican site.

As you read the propaganda from any site, you will be able to feel your flesh rising within you. Be aware of your blood pressure and learn to associate with 'what' your anger is being brought about by.

If you are married, listen to your body language as you and your spouse engage in conflict. Are you crossing your arms? Rolling your eyes? Again, Mussar is an action and learning what your body is telling you before you even know it will help you prepare for reactions.

Acknowledge: I am angry right now. The cycle is beginning.

Resist: Get away from the person/object/cause that you think is making you angry. Take a walk. Take a breather. Take a shower.

Reverse it: Come back into the room a different person. This takes work. Who said it was going to be easy? Come back into the situation calm, lacking in rage, able to communicate. Force yourself to be still and listen to God. He will not tell you to scream, hit, yell, or throw things. He will tell you to be still.

You can do this.

Nothing is so great that God is perplexed

Patience

In your patience possess you your souls. Luke 21:19

This is my Achilles tendon. This is my flu bug, my baggage. Patience, impatience, they both strap together.

My niece has patience that I covet. She has 5 children under the age of 13 and home schools. She can laugh over anything! The two boys are fighting and she can break it up with a smile on her face. I love talking to her on the phone; there is always laughter.

What is so interesting is that we come from the same blood- line. Her dad, my brother has little tolerance for anyone, he can be very impatient. My dad had almost no patience and I struggle with impatience. Yet, here comes my niece, laughing and carrying on. She has great patience!

I have heard it said that so and so has a lot of patience until they snap and then its, boy, look out! But is that really patience at all? Doesn't it more resemble a kind of impatience? "I'm fine until you push all my buttons, or until you push *that* button then I snap!....so look out and don't push me!" That's impatience and arrogance to the core.

A person with patience wouldn't snap, for they wouldn't let it get that far.

Having patience is one of those calming keys that we so desire. To lose one's patience usually ends in anger, which causes stress in our lives, hardening of the arteries, and possibly a shorter life.

One of the most important exercises is discovering *why* we might lose our patience. Do we lose it quickly, or do we build and build until we snap? Is it a certain item, the phone, the computer, the washing machine? Is it traffic, or a bad driver in front of you or a tail gaiter behind you? Is it a person coughing behind you at the movie theater? Is it the long lines at the airport and you're running late and ahead of you is a mommy with a stroller, a baby, a two year old and a five year old boy jumping all over the place?

Pray for a while, contemplate on it, and write it down. Go through this next week writing events down that trigger your impatience. "I am patient until…"

Pray about your code word or words that will bring you back to the reality of the situation. Once you snap, you are no longer living in the reality of the moment. You have gone into the: me, myself and I cyberspace. Suddenly the whole thing revolves around you. "Oh, she's making *me* late…." "Oh, great, *I'm* going to get sick…"or "This blankety blank computer is going to ruin *my* paper…" or "Oh, this lady's bugging *me*, she's going so slow!"

Alan Morinis tells his readers that when we are in a situation that is triggering our impatience, instead of finding fault with that person, we can choose to be patient and take responsibility for our reactions. He teaches to 'call' on patience as a tangible thing. We make a choice whether we crumble under the situation or take dominion over the situation. Mr. Morinis tells us that his teacher Rabbi Perr calls this awareness: "opening the space between the match and the fuse."[1]

My daughter and I were to be somewhere at a specific time. She was 17 at the moment and took a very substantial amount of time preparing to go out of the house. I'm over 50, short hair due to chemo, hardly any eyelashes and so it doesn't take me long at all. I waited and waited, periodically calling to her, "Come on, we're going to be late!" Well, when she finally came down, I was livid, I had lost my patience. Granted, she should be respectful of the person that we had agreed to meet at a certain time, and we've worked on that. But, at that time, did it do any good for me to lose my patience? No, I just added stress to my body; in fact I soon left the character trait of impatience and became angry. I had lost it.

Of course there are times when patience is not a virtue, if a speedy reaction would involve someone's' life and help is a necessity. But we all know the difference between acting quickly to assist someone and what this chapter is all about.

Patience in Hebrew is *tsavlanut,* which can also mean tolerance. In the book *Cheshbon ha'Nefesh*, Rabbi Leffin tells his readers: "Woe to the pampered one who has never been trained to be patient. Either today or in the future he is destined to sip from the cup of affliction."[2]

My code words for patience were, 'listen…breathe.' These two words made me stop and be still and gain composure of myself. How can I be yelling or losing my patience at someone or something if I am stopping, listening and breathing? I have had to learn the hard way that losing my patience rarely if ever makes things happen faster.

Patience is a giving attribute. Impatience is a very self- centered character trait. When one loses their patience they are solely concerned with self. The Father and His Son are the greatest examples of patience. Even though we seem to have exhausted every measure of patience and kindness to others, God has patience and our lives are sustained. He gives us time to redeem ourselves and to start over. Forgiveness plays a big part in impatience. Saying merely I'm sorry to the one we may have snapped at goes a long way.

"*I waited patiently for YHWH and He inclined to me and heard my cry*". Psalms *Tehillin* 40:1. Isn't that remarkable? He waited for The Lord.

"*And it shall be said in that day, See, this is our Elohim. We have waited for Him and He saves us. This is YHWH, we have waited for Him, let us be glad and rejoice in His deliverance.*" Isaiah *Yeshayahu* 25:9

"*The end of the matter is better than its beginning. The patient in spirit is better than the proud in spirit.*" Ecclesiastics *Qoheleth* 7:8

These verses tell us something that goes against the grain of mankind. That we must wait. We are a culture, a nation of hurry ups. I remember I was so thrilled to get the Internet, to finally see what everyone was talking about. But, living out in area that we do, we have dial up. There was a time when that was sufficient, but now it's slow. We need the information faster!

No longer do we open our Bibles or songbooks. Now it's right there in front of our eyes on the slide. Instant words! Instant songs!

I really don't have to cook anymore, I can buy everything prepackaged, even challa bread.

Technology is a very good thing. Information is a great thing. Knowledge is power. But wisdom in The Lord is best, for wisdom, is His and gives honor in return, and we glorify Him in the end. Those verses mentioned tell us, His children, to wait on Him, be patient for Him. Not Him to wait on me, although in His mercy He does. So, when I am not patient with one of His children, I am not waiting on Him, but expecting Him to conform to my desires. Now.

Rabbi Sha'ul, Paul, in the book of 2Timothy, tells us to follow his teachings. What teachings was he referring to? He was a Rabbi from the tribe of Benjamin and was learned of Rabbi Gamliel, so what teachings would he be referring to? God's instruction, His character, His 613 principles of life. The Torah.

"*But you did closely follow my teaching, the way of life, the purpose, the belief, the patience, the love, the endurance…*" 2Timothy 3:10

"*My brothers, count it all joy when you fall into various trials, knowing that the proving of your belief works endurance, and let endurance have a perfect work so that you may be perfect and complete, lacking in nothing."* James 1:2-4

In the book of James, we are admonished to be patient until the Messiah comes. That is the great coming of The Lord, whom we all want to come. Quickly. But we are told to be patient, how much more then should I be patient with my brothers and sisters. *"So, brothers, be patient until the coming of the Master. See, the farmer waits for the precious fruit of the earth, waiting patiently for it until it receives the early and latter rain. You too, be patient. Establish your hearts; for the coming of the Master has drawn hear. Do not grumble against each other brothers, lest you be judged. See the Judge is standing at the door! My brothers, as an example of suffering and patience take the prophets, who spoke in the Name of YHWH."* James 5:7-10

Those verses are fantastic – comparing patience to a farmer. Would the fruit grow faster if farmer went out and yelled at the tree? Would the grass be greener if he stomped in the house and slammed the door?

Being ranchers here in Southwestern Colorado, we have to put up hay for the winter for the livestock. Jay irrigates from May through October, and usually gets two cuttings. Irrigating the old way is an art. It reminds me of The Father and His word.

As Jay opens up the head gates, water pours down the ditch and through the cuts that Jay and the boys have made to water the fields. The fields drink and change. Within a day red wing black birds are everywhere, and the sound of calling frogs echoes on our land. The fields come alive. Baby calves run and play with their tails straight up and foals run and run.

But days and days go by, with Jay doing the same process. Cut a ditch here, close a line there, water this part, and dry off that part. Again and again, throughout the days until the grass is just right. Patience. Jay wants the best yield for the cutting, whether it's the first, second, third or only cutting. It takes patience.

The Messiah Yeshua spoke in Luke 21:19, *"Possess your lives by your endurance."*

"Here is the patience of the set apart ones, here are those guarding the commands of Elohim and the belief of Yeshua." Revelation 14:12

We are given patience when we pray for patience. But we have to have a trial to develop patience and endurance. Our patience comes from living in God's Word and the belief of Yeshua/Jesus as the Messiah.

If patience comes from The Father, and it does; then it is spiritual. We breathe, we think, we contemplate, we visualize then we react. Impatience is physical, a human fleshly reaction to a given situation. We pant, we scream, our blood pressure goes up, we cuss, we throw things, we yell. Patience/Spiritual vs. Impatience/Physical.

You will have ample opportunity to express your patience in this week. The Father will give you opportunities to refine yourself, for His Glory; at work, at home, on the road, in the classroom and at church/synagogue. Romans 5:3

Be careful with words and thoughts that begin with 'you'. 'You make me so mad..' or 'You're making me late…"

In *Cheshbon HaNefesh*, Rabbi Mendel starts out his chapter on patience with two very wise sentences. He tells his readers that when something bad happens to us, and we did not have the power to avoid it, to not heighten the situation even more by wasted grief. [3]

He also says that God's perfection is glorified in this world in three ways, through His ability, through His wisdom and through His grace, which is granted without hidden motive. [4]

Be aware of idle thoughts that will push you towards a belief that you are right and the driver in front of you is wrong. They are going slow, or slower, maybe, but does that make them wrong? God's grace is sufficient for all, and if you pray, if you stop and think and pray about the situation, He will get you there at the place that you must be, in time. But if you lose your patience and get mad at one of His children just because they are driving slower, you have taken the Grace out of His hands and replaced it with condemnation and a very self-centered attitude. You have become the very focus of yourself – ego – instead of God being the center of it all.

Impatience is really the scene behind self-centeredness. When one becomes impatient with another human being we are really elevating ourselves above that person. The situation doesn't matter, whether you are trying to get into an elevator and there is a very slow person in front of you, or a person in a check out line with three carts, or a person stalled at a green light. Whatever the situation is, even with your children or spouse, when we lose our patience we elevate our being above those that 'just made us so mad we lost our patience'.

To have patience is a reversal; it is to elevate the person above ourselves. It is to bear that other person's burden, to understand, to listen and to have compassion. We are giving that person the better seat at the wedding.

Patience is the key to inner peace and impatience is the deterioration of the soul. [5]

Examples:

"Dear God, this person is driving way too slow, I'm afraid I'll be late for my doctor's appointment. Please give me grace to be patient with this person and grace to make my appointment on time." Now take a deep breath and chant, or sing, or hum.

Your child just spilled milk all over the Sabbath lace tablecloth and the phone is ringing, the dog is scratching at the door and the baby is screaming.

"Dear God, give me grace to smile at my child, after all it *is* just a table cloth. And thank you for the grace you've allowed me." Now breathe, clean up the mess, hug your child, pick up the baby, let the dog in and don't answer the phone.

You can do this, I know you can. Get your code word or words, and remember to write in your journal every night, taking heed to the things that trigger your 'patience' button. Write down what made you snap, and look for situations for the following day that you can use to work on.

1. Everyday Holiness The Path of Mussar, Alan Morinis
2. Cheshbon HaNefesh
3. Cheshbon HaNefesh
4. Cheshbon HaNefesh
5. Pastor Jay Howard, Simchat haMashiach Beit Emunah

Change Your Life

<u>Notes</u> <u>Week Two</u> <u>Patience</u>

Code word or words:

Situations to recognize:

<u>*Patience:*</u>

Day One

Day Two

Day Three

Day Four

Day Five

Day Six

Day Seven

The Exercise:
For patience/impatience you will have to again, create a situation that would cause you to lose your patience. No one knows that better than you, and it is very important to be honest with yourself. Is it something burning? Maybe you work on dinner all afternoon and then purposely let it burn – test your patience. Is it the computer? You might have to work on a project or an in-depth letter and allow the computer to actually eat it.

What is important here is that you are conscious of impatience slowly creeping into your character.

Find the code word that works for you and repeat it. Remember that Mussar is an action, and by creating a controlled situation that would have ordinarily caused you to lose your patience, you become aware of the areas around you. Impatience is a physical act, don't forget that. So before you physically react to a problem, a situation that is driving you nuts and you are about to lose your patience, remember the spiritual aspect. Breathe, count, sing, hum, say your code words, pray.

And it's okay to blow it, don't give up.

While heading down to the barn to do the morning chores, a very small thing happened to almost make me lose my patience. In fact, I could literally feel my cheeks getting red. I'm training myself to look for the signs, to feel the signs and they were there.

I was driving to the barn with the water (we haul water in the winter) and ahead of me were the two boys, the four dogs and our 20 year old daughter. She was home this particular day and helping.

The middle boy was being crazy, goofy, out of control, a pest, ornery, and just plain obnoxious to the other two. Now, remember, I'm watching all of this as they are a ways ahead of me down the snow packed road.

I see the middle boy picking on the other two, throwing snowballs, pushing them in the snow, pushing them down in the snow, etc. All of a sudden the other two ganged up on the middle boy, pushed him down in the snow and as he is gleefully screaming – the younger boy throws a snow ball in his face and it gets sucked down into his throat. Instantly all the hoopla and fun stop and the middle boy is now beet red and choking. The party's over and I'm mad.

But, I didn't lose my composure – quite. I practiced Mussar.

And if I can do it – you can, too!

You can do it. Acknowledge – resist – reverse.

2Peter 1:5-6
Colossians 1:9-11
James 1:3
Breathe.
Recognize – repent – renounce – resist – reverse

Recognize: My heart is beating faster, I'm walking faster, I know I'm mad.

Repent: Stop, I'm sorry I am thinking about losing my patience.

Renounce: I am not going to lose my patience – I renounce it.

Resist: Code Words or Scripture verse.

Reverse: Instead of yelling I show compassion on the middle boy as well as the other two who obviously feel very bad that they threw the snowball and it went down his throat.

Breathe again.

Love is patient love is kind

Joy

"Sing aloud to God our strength and make a joyful noise to the God of Jacob."
Psalms *Tehillim* 81:1

When you research the word 'joy' in a concordance, you will be overwhelmed and amazed. The words joy, peace, God, Lord, joyful, rejoice, soul and salvation all seem to be connected. They tie into each other, and without one another, it is almost impossible to have the other. You can't have peace without joy, and you can't have joy without peace and you can't have peace without God and you can't have The Messiah without salvation and you can't be joyful without peace, without joy, without The Lord. It just won't work.

Joy can illustrate a wedding, as in Jeremiah 25:10, and festivities, too. But mostly the word Joy is *in* the Lord with Holy Days, as in Numbers 10:10, which are sacred occasions of many types.

In the Hebrew language, *Simchat*, translates as joy forty four times, gladness thirty one times, mirth eight times, rejoice three times, rejoicing twice, and other meanings six times. It has also been translated as the "happiness we share."

Some may debate that The Lord is not a necessary element of joy. An opinion may be that they have joy. In what, I wonder. In their children, their job, their sports, their friends? That's not really joy. It can be satisfaction, or excitement, or fun, or love or pride or pleasure. Drinking and eating are pleasures too; these are pleasures of the flesh. Swimming is relaxing; reading is good for the brain, and taking a walk is healthy for our bodies. But true joy comes from The Father, His Word and His salvation, which in turn gives us His Peace. His Shalom. True joy is when one has been fulfilled.[1]

"Your words were found and I did eat them and the word was to me the joy and rejoicing of my heart for I am called by the name, O Lord God of hosts."
Jeremiah *Yirmeyahu* 15:16

Jeremiah is telling The Father that His Word *becomes* joy.

"Be glad in the Lord and rejoice you righteous: and shout for joy all you that are upright in hearts. Psalms *Tehillim* 32:11

David is telling us to shout for joy for we are glad *in* The Lord.

"You will show me the path of life: in your presence is fullness of joy, at the right hand there are pleasures forever more." Psalm, *Tehillim* 16:11

This is a remarkable statement by King David. First, he is proclaiming that God will show us the path of light, (His Word, the Torah,...*Your word is a lamp to my feet...*). Then, David is stating that in God's presence is the fullness of joy, (fullness: richness, completeness, flavor, tastiness, extensiveness, detail, breadth, comprehensiveness).

The last part of the declaration is that at the right hand of The Father there are pleasures forever more. And who is seated at the right hand of The Father? Who has the power and the glory? Our Messiah, Yeshua. He is where our pleasure is forever more. That is true Joy.

Through the Messiah we are given the Spirit, *"But the fruit of the spirit is love, joy, peace, long suffering, gentleness, goodness, faith..."* Galatians 5:22

Joy in Hebrew is *Simcha, Simchah, Simchat*. The root, s'-m-h denotes being glad or joyful with the whole character as indicated by connection with the heart: Exodus 4:14, Psalms 19:8, Psalms 104:15, and Psalms 105:3. The soul: Psalms 86:4, and with the lighting up with the eye; Proverbs 15:30. [2]

"I have no greater joy than to hear that my children walk in truth." 3John 4

"For what is our hope, or joy, or crown of rejoicing, is it not even you in the presence of our Lord Yeshua The Messiah at His coming?" 1Thessalonians 2:19

"For you are our glory and joy." 1Thessalonians 2:20

"I rejoiced greatly that I have found some of your children walking in truth as we received commandments from The Father." 2John 4.

Rabbi Shau'l(Paul) and Yochannan, (John) are impressing upon us that joy is a direct link to truth, which is The Word and The Messiah. They go hand in hand.

Truth/joy/God/Torah/Yeshua.

Holidays, good times, skiing, walking, and reading can bring you good memories and warm feelings. But true and pure joy comes only from The Father, His Word and His Salvation, His Son. Nothing else. It is an inner joy coming from The Source.

When I prepare for one of The Fathers' Holy Days, I am in complete joy. There is no stress, I don't have to worry about finances, God always provides enough to have a special dinner, for His appointed Days. I never have to go into debt; I don't have to fight the crowds in any store. Even if the meal is simply a baked potato, it is coming from Him. He is sustaining me, which is His Joy. Therefore it becomes my joy, a complete feeling of peace and joy that I am looking forward to one of The Holy Days and sharing it with The Father and The Son.

"*O Come let us sing to The Lord, let us make a joyful noise to the rock of our salvation.*" Psalms 95:1

And who is The Rock of Salvation? Yeshua. Joy is the quintessence of faith.

The Ways of the Tzaddikim explain that to worry over the affairs of this world is reprehensible and is not found in those who trust in God. "Worry and sorrow erode the heart and are the sickness of the body. The worst of all worries is pursuing transgressions and worrying and suffering in not attaining all his heart's desires for all who worry and grieve over this world are very far from Torah, mitzvos, and prayer."[3]

What is worry. To be anxious, to fret, to be troubled, and to agonize. When I think of worrying, I think of wringing of the hands, or pacing. I think of sweating and shortness of breath. I also think of nothing accomplished.

When I was diagnosed with stage IIIB breast cancer, my body wanted to fly into a panic mode. The s-word came right to my mind and it flew out my mouth. I wanted to run, to escape, and to worry. That reaction was trying to give way to fear and doubt and stress. And those reactions would only cause greater sickness.[4] Worry is not an emotion, it is a reaction to a certain cause, and it is never the ends to a mean. Worry never will bring you to a conclusion. To worry is to dwell on the consequences of things going wrong, [5] but in whose mindset?

I cried and then I prayed and then I called my husband. He prayed, and called Rabbi Messer and he prayed. The substance of prayer gave me, maybe them too, calmness, a peace and a sense of joy, in the strangest way. I am certainly not trying to convince anyone that there is joy in cancer. It's a club I didn't want to join, and never thought I would, but due to consequences and generational curses, I was made a honorary member.

Somehow, God sustained me and I was able to find joy in Him. I knew His presence was before me, like the cloud and the fire. He was already going through anything I had to face, and He would never leave me. Trusting in Him, released the worry and gave me peace, calmness and joy.

Getting chemo wasn't a happy thing, but meeting the people, the nurses, and talking with the other women gave me a sense of joy. I am richer now in life for having met those people, they touched my life and I touched theirs. I have more joy now for I cherish it more. Do I want worry in my life or joy? If you worry as a rule, redirect your thinking; let us ask ourselves, why do I worry? Why am I worrying?

The Ways of the Tzaddikim, write of tears coming from sorrow and worry. *"My eyes have shed streams of tears for not having observed your Torah."* Psalms *Tehillim* 119:136. And for worry Psalms 38:18 is quoted. In *The Scriptures*, [6] the publishers use the word 'sorry'. *"For I confess my crookedness, I am sorry over my sin."* Psalms *Tehillim* 38:18.

To be sorry or to have remorse over something is a different concept than to worry. Yet it can be the direct cause of my worrying. If I have said something that I think may have offended someone, I am sorry over that. I can most certainly contact that person and be quick to ask forgiveness. If I worry over the sin of gossip, I have neither solved the problem, healed the heart of that person nor for that matter, healed my own heart. Worry will keep me dormant in that season.

Yeshua, in the book of Matthew, is very explicit about His children worrying. *"Therefore I tell you, do not worry about your life, what you will eat or drink; or about your body, what you will wear. Is not life more important than food and the body more important than clothes? Look at the birds of the air; they do not sow or reap or store away in barns, and yet your heavenly Father feeds them. Are you not much more valuable than they? Who of you by worrying can add a single hour to his life? And why do you worry about clothes? See how the lilies of the field grow. They do not labor or spin. Yet I tell you that not even Solomon in all his splendor was dressed like one of these. If that is how God clothes the grass of the field, which is here today and tomorrow is thrown into the fire, will He not much more clothe you, O you of little faith? So do not worry saying, 'What shall we eat?' or 'What shall we drink?' or 'What shall we wear?' For the pagans run after all these things, and your heavenly Father knows that you need them. But seek first His kingdom and His righteousness, and all these things will be given to you as well. Therefore do not worry about tomorrow, for tomorrow will worry about itself. Each day has enough trouble of its own."* Matthew *Mattithyahu*, 6:25-34.[7]

It is silly and ridiculous to think that this statement means to sit on ones rear and look to the sky for a jug of milk. No, Yeshua is not telling us to be lazy, but rather not to worry. He likens worry to the practices of pagans; Rabbi Sha'ul calls them 'once gentiles'. They worry for they have no God, no end. We have the strength and the power to not worry, for our strength is not our own – it is in Him.

As you progress through this week, make notes of what causes you worry and make an analytical thought to replace that despairing feeling with joy, *Simchat*. Study through the verses in Equanimity and what your thought processes were during that and rise above the situations that cause worry. Wake each morning in the joy that you are alive and have been given one more day to express your love to The Father.

Daniel Botkin in one of his newsletters said that he was soon to turn sixty. He found joy in that as he greeted each new decade with thanks and gratefulness. 'I didn't die in my forties! I didn't die in my 50's!' [8]. What joy!

There are three elements needed for complete joy. They are free, non cumbersome, non burdensome, non legalistic, and very easy to acquire.

1. The Father
2. His Word
3. His Son

May your joy be full in them.

1. Pastor Jay Howard, Simchat haMashiach Beit Emunah
2. Logos, Bible Software
3. The Ways of the Tzaddikim
4. Simchat Torah Beit Midrash, Mrs. Maureen Messer, the Mikveh Service, Denver CO.
5. Pastor Jay Howard Simchat haMashiach Beit Emunah
6. The Scriptures, Institute for Scripture Research
7. The Holy Bible, NIV
8. Daniel Botkin, Gates of Eden, Peoria IL.

Notes *Week Three* *Joy*

Code word or words:

Situations to recognize:

Joy:

Day One:

Day Two:

Day Three:

Day Four:

Day Five:

Day Six:

Day Seven:

The Exercise:

Worry is self-inflicted. I believe that worry is given to us that we may strive to attain joy. There is a huge difference from being prepared and worrying.

As ranchers, we often have the unfortunate experience of losing calves in the winter when they are born. Many nights we would lay awake and worry if a calf was being born during the blizzard, or if a calf was even okay. The blizzard and temperatures were often so severe that we could humanly do nothing. We did what we could, but so many sad times we would find a calf frozen in a ditch, or half dead after the blizzard. Worrying didn't save that calf. But, when we changed our worry to preparedness we changed the situations within us.

What makes you worry? Is it health? Money? Your children? Is it the future of our country? Truly seek out in your life what makes you worry, and then find knowledge in that through seeking the wisdom from the Torah.

If it is the economy, seek God's wisdom in that. Really try to get out of debt, cut up a credit card. Start small. Eat pintos for dinner. Do you worry about your health? Find God's wisdom in that. Exercise, eat better. Reduce your smoking (if you smoke) start small. Breathe deep – take a walk.

Find the source that makes you worry and ask yourself what it is about that particular thing that actually makes you worry. For instance, can you really do anything about the economy? No, but you can prepare for certain things in your private economy. Really search the reasons why you worry.

Now, to find joy. But is joy lost? What in your life gives you joy? I know that for my mother it is her three children. She is quite elderly and her world has shrunk to her home and her children. Friends are good and bring her happiness, but the joy that she finds in her children, are boundless. She thanks The Lord for her children, for that joy comes from Him as her children were gifts of Him.

Whatever it is, start by thanking The Lord for giving you that joy. For joy first must come from Him, in Him and through Him. *Baruch Ata Adonai.*

When worry creeps into your life like a cockroach, smash it. Kill it. Replace it with just one single thought of joy. Baby steps, you can do it.

Rejoice in YHWH always, again, I say rejoice! Let your gentleness be known to all men, The Master is near. Do not worry at all, but by every matter by prayer and petition with thanksgiving, let your requests be made known to Elohim.
Philippians 4:4-7

Order

Order is the accurate arrangement of all things. 1

In Numbers 2, YHWH is very precise in exactly how He desires the tribes to camp. In the book of Revelation, chapters 4 and 7, God is very clear in His order regarding the tribes and numbers. They are symmetrical to each other. The same is East, West, North and South.

In the story of creation, The Father has a specific order to His Creation. He had to have an order, it couldn't be random, it wouldn't work. And after each day, what are we told? That it was good. And the order of the Sabbath, so strategically placed at the end of our workweek, so we, His beloved creations could rest with Him and in Him.

The seven covenants of God are stacked upon one another bringing order to one another. If one is removed, or 'done away' with, the rest of the covenants will lose that part of the foundation. If one believes that there is only one covenant, then they must be hallucinating whenever they see a rainbow. These seven covenants are just another example of the order of The Father. When we realize the importance of order in God, we can begin to see the importance of it in our lives.

The seven covenants are:

1. Eden
2. Adamic
3. Noahdic
4. Abrahamic
5. Mosaic
6. Davidic
7. Renewed

God creates order, man creates chaos. *Kol 'b Seder* in Hebrew means 'everything is in order'. A *Seder* is the order of Passover. You can't drink the fourth cup before you partake in the first cup. In *Everyday Holiness the Path of Mussar*, 2 Alan Morinis gives an example of Rabbi Dessler's three reasons why we should make an effort to bring order into our lives. First, the knowing that things are arranged creates a feeling of personal satisfaction and assurance that every thing is under control. The second reason is practicality; order helps us find things when we need them and saves us time. The third reason is that many things of the world will only function if arranged and put in order correctly. Have you ever tried to sew with a sewing machine and the order of the thread was incorrect? It won't work.

The cycle of The Torah and the cycle of the Feast days are an order of the universe. If we aren't in God's sync, we will have dis-order. We may think that everything in our lives is in order, but what we have created is a man made arrangement of a man made order. The Scriptures tell us to seek the Kingdom of God first and the rest will fall into place. The careful interpretation of that Scripture will tell us that it is God's Kingdom, His Torah, His 613 principles, that we are to seek, not a duplicate or replica of that Kingdom that a system has put into place.

In Leviticus, *Wayyiqra* chapter 23, God tells us what His order is. *"And YHWH spoke to Moses saying, Speak to the children of Israel and say to them, the appointed times of YHWH which you are to proclaim as set apart gatherings, My appointed times are these: ..."*

God goes on to inform us about His Sabbath and the Holy Days. Yeshua, in the plan of His life followed these Holy Days, and He is these High Holy Days. He is our rest, He is and was the Passover, He is the First Fruit, and the unleavened bread. He is the Holy Spirit, Shavout/Pentecost and He will come with the shout of the trumpet, He is the atonement for all who trust in Him. He tabernacles with us in our lives today and will once again physically tabernacle with all.

Order in the universe is nothing we as a people can create. Can we rearrange the order of the sun and the moon and the stars? We can change the Holy Days to holidays, but we can not change the fact that the Sabbath is the seventh Day.

In the book of Numbers, chapter nine, YHWH is covering His people with a cloud by day and fire by night.

"And so it was, when the cloud dwelt only from evening until morning, when the cloud was taken up in the morning then they departed.

Whether by day or by night, whenever the cloud was taken up, they departed. Whether two days, or a month, or a year that the cloud lingered above the Dwelling Place to dwell upon it, the children of Yisre'el camped and did not depart. But when it was taken up, they departed.

At the command of YHWH, they camped and at the command of YHWH they departed. They guarded the Charge of YHWH at the command of YHWH by the hand of Mosheh."

Order. God's order. To camp or not to camp was not the choice of any council, person, belief, program or community. It was the order of God.

Order in our life will come from The Father, but only if we submit our will to His – totally. Alan Morinis says that being a servant of God means striving to align our will to that of The Master. Rabbi Gamliel, the Rabbi of Shau'l, put it so plainly; 'Do His will as if it were your will that He may do your will as if it were His will.'

It is also impossible to be 'the likeness' of The Master with out the order of The Father, for Yeshua has no disorder in His Life or in His Word and He is the Likeness of The Father. You can try to arrange your own order, but it is God's order that our very souls seek.

Order in our house in certain areas can come from a little bit of diligence. We can have order in our kitchens, garages, closets, and desks. But order in our families and our spiritual home, again can only come from The Father.

If you find that your house, your life is out of order, really seek The Fathers' guidance. Ask Him to show you and then accept the truth that He will give.

Order in our everyday duties however, can be corrected. Start with the closet. Clean it out, hang it up, fold it away. Start at your desk, file it, staple it, and throw it away. How about the garage or the kitchen? Without order in these areas, we are bound to be wasting something, whether it is your time, your resources or someone else's time and resources. Even in regards to relationships, it is important to have order.

Almost everyone has heard the saying: Let's do lunch. If that statement was true, and the lunch date was followed through, then there is order. But if that statement was flippantly said to another, and chaos or busyness has kept the lunch from happening, then order is not in that persons' life. Days, weeks, months have slipped by…and no phone call and no lunch. It's a small statement, and a popular one. Is it a true one?

In the order of the universe, the Sabbath is the seventh day. There is no changing the fact that the Sabbath, the seventh day in the order of creation is the Holy Day of The Lord, the Day of Rest. Lives can seem to be in order, and everything going smoothly, but until the order of The Lord is implemented in the life of an individual, order is not fully present. It is amazing how order will present itself just by realizing that The Father has the best plan for order in our lives.

Seeking His order first, will help to bring order into our everyday affairs. The first chapter in the character traits is equanimity, which is to rise above all things. Order in a house can slip off into chaos if we allow analytical order to control our life instead of God's order. We can have all our ducks in a row, but if we are not in God's Order we are actually in disorder.

We are living in a busy world, and life happens. We may be in order to leave for the market, an interview, our job, church, whatever and something happens. A child smashes his finger in the door, the muddy dog jumps up on our clean clothes, the baby soils his pants, the phone rings and it's your mother wanting to talk. Anything can bring a sense of disorder into our schedule.

Being in order can be a fine line. Be wise in differentiating the order that we thought we deserved in that moment of time, and the order that The Father so graciously gives us. There is an order of man, and there is the never-ending order of the Father that is so crucial for us to have in our lives.

Could we possible be so presumptuous to think that our own created order is better than Gods'? If He has created the Sabbath, the 7th Day as His orderly day of rest, how can man possibly that think by changing it to the first day of the week, it would be better. Chaos begins.

Could laziness be the opposite of order? Clothes on the floor, shirts not hung up, dishes piled in the sink, the TV constantly on, trash in the car, desks piled in a heap, bills scattered among magazines on the dining room table, cars with dirty oil, etc. Laziness can be too much TV, not looking for employment, not willing or wanting to work. Laziness can be not calling someone back, or in our world, not answering an email.

Laziness can be disguised as our comfort zone. We want to be a couch potato, sometimes we don't want out of it, maybe it would be too much work to get out of it, or too spiritually challenging. We want to stay in that church in that particular pew forever and nod our heads, then go home and eat ham.

"*The lazy one is wiser in his own eyes. Than seven rendering advice.*" Proverbs, *Mishle* 26:16

It takes effort and time and order to study God's Word and seek His Wisdom. It takes order to implement His Will in our lives. His will is that we do not eat certain foods. Might it sometimes be easier to just eat that bacon at the breakfast than seek out something different? Subsequently, that bacon may put our bodies out of order.

In studying history with my third grader, there was such a good example of laziness when the first party from England arrived on the Eastern Coast. They weren't prepared and some of the pilgrims chose not to work. Most of the new Americans starved, froze and died that first winter. What a classic example of wanting something, but not willing to put it in order.

The Scriptures are full of examples and quotes in regards to laziness. The one most often quoted, especially to our children, is proverbs. *"But if you closely consider the ants, they are very much in order."* Proverbs *Mishle* 6:6-11. Millions of tiny ants going here and there, each one having a certain job and in complete order. Just like the beehive. What complexity yet what order! They couldn't survive without that immense type of order. And The Father gave it to them. Just as He wants to give us order. *"And He spoke this parable. 'A certain man had a fig tree planted in his vineyard and he came seeking fruit on it and found none. And he said to the gardener, 'Look, for three years I have come seeking fruit on this fig tree and find none. Cut it down, why does it even make the ground useless?' And he answering said to Him, 'Master, leave it this year too, until I dig around it and throw manure. And if indeed it bears fruit, good, but if not so you shall cut it down.'"* Luke 13:6-9

Very plainly, a tree that doesn't bear fruit is cut down. Our fruit that we bear is in The Fathers' plan, not our plan. I would argue with anyone that does not believe that His order is perfect and mans is faulty. The Fathers' seasons are perfect, mans are faulty. In fact, in most of the states we actually have to set our clocks in different order for two of the seasons. We have changed The Fathers New Year; we have changed the timing of His Days and seasons. We have in a sense tried to reconstruct His Order. But to live in order is to live in accordance to the Holy One who made us, [3] – to accept His plan of life and salvation.

Alan Morinis teaches that within order are two soul traits that can be negated or amplified, humility and honor. It is human nature to rebel against order, as in the example of Moses explaining to YHWH that there would be grumblings amongst the camp in regards to the order of the arrangement that God had chosen for the tribes to camp around the Tabernacle. This attitude then always involved a 'me, myself and I' concept. Therefore a lack of humility. The lack of honor, *kavod*, shows up in the disorder that we may have in our lives, house, job, etc. By being sloppy, lazy, or disorderly we are not honoring the person we work with, or live with. These are all self-based issues. Honor is due all persons, it is not ours to judge who should be honored or not because of their greatness or achievements, but more simply because they are in turn a holy soul and we are not to judge the Divine One's plan.[4]

In fact, we have lacked honor and humility towards The Father by recreating His order. *"Therefore, YHWH of Israel declares, I said indeed that your house and the house of your father would walk before Me forever. But now YHWH declares, Far be it from Me, for those who honor Me I honor and those who despise Me I do not honor."* 1Samuel *1Shemu'el* 2:30. Since God created the earth and the heavens for His own glory and He repays honor with honor, surely, we can do the same. We can be in order.

When we are in total chaos, our very beings cry for order. You will know if you are out of order, we can feel the chaos upon us like a heavy blanket. Sometimes we feel out of control, spinning around like a child's top and we can't stop the motion. That is where, again, we breathe. Take five minutes and stop, breathe, listen, pray. Take baby steps. Start with a kitchen drawer. Work towards the closet or garage. Completely reorganize a filing cabinet. Line shirts up by color. You will find that the more you acquire order, the more our beings, our very souls relax and seem to sprout. Take baby steps and realize that your spirit craves order. But trying to get in order can give us chaos. Go slow, pray.

Order can begin simply by praying every morning at a set time. We can set the alarm for fifteen minutes earlier to rise, pray and praise The Father and breathe.

We are alive for His Glory, to give Him Praise and Honor. Order will come, be patient, it will come.

1. Rabbi Ralph Messer, Simchat Torah Beit Midrash, Denver CO
2. Everyday Holiness, The Path of Mussar, Alan Morinis
3. Pastor Jay Howard Simchat haMashiach Beit Emunah
4. Everyday Holiness, The Path of Mussar, Alan Morinis

Change Your Life

<u>Notes</u>　　　　　<u>Week Four</u>　　　　　<u>Order</u>

Code word or words:

Situations to recognize:

Order:

Day One:

Day Two:

Day Three:

Day Four:

Day Five:

Day Six:

Day Seven:

The Exercise:

Order is a state of balance between chaos and compulsion. The books that are piled upon the desk, is it necessary to have them in alphabetical order on your shelf? Probably not.

The shirts in your closet are they thrown over one another, hung up neatly or arranged by colors. Look at the cabinet in the kitchen where you keep those plastic bowls. Do you have a hundred lids and only 5 bowls? Is it important to you that they are arranged by size? Or do you throw them under the sink?

If you are a not so orderly person, start small. Begin with one drawer, one shelf, one closet and get it in order. Throw out what you haven't used, or give it away.

Sometimes when we clean a closet, it leads to the painting of the hall. Ever been there? And then life seems totally overwhelming. So, keep focused on the closet. Do the hall next month.

Are you disorderly with your friends? Keep in mind that to honor them is a Mussar teaching of order. Do not be late for appointments either with your friends or professional people that you must see. In the honor of other people that you come in contact with, you will be setting order in your life.

Rabbi Messer of Simchat Torah Beit Midrash, Denver CO teaches that if someone isn't respectful of your time they aren't respectful of you. Switch that around, and honor someone else's time in this world. Honor their space, and you will find that your space gains order as you try to accomplish honor for your neighbor/friend/spouse/child. *Kol b'seder:* everything is in order.

"Despise not any man and discard not anything, for there is not a man who has not his hour and there exists not a thing which has not its place." *Pirkei Avos, Ethics of the Fathers.*

If you are not in sink with God's Appointed Times, you are still is disorder, not matter how well your shirts are lined up. No matter how hard you try, there will be dis- order in your life. Seek His Wisdom, study His High Holy Days. Who is anyone on this planet to tell God, 'Oh, I think I'll do it this way, thank you very much.' I urge you, with your spouse if you are married, to really look at the Hebrew order of the universe. The cycle of His Times, the cycle of life. You will be amazed, and order in everything will begin to creep into your life. Seek His Kingdom first.

Just begin, you can do this.

Kol b' seder.

He made the moon for appointed times.
   Psalm 104:19

Truth

The Truth shall set you free.

The signature of The Holy Blessed One is truth. Shabbat 55a

Truth in Hebrew is *Emet* and is an amazing concept. Truth has been mistaken and replaced by the opinions and perceptions of man.

CNN has a different truth than FOX. Democrats have their truth, Republicans have theirs. Different countries have differing truths. The Catholic Church has a different truth than a Baptist Church as will the Methodist denominations. A Messianic Synagogue will perceive a different truth than an orthodox Synagogue as will a Reformed Synagogue. The Ute People will have their truth; the Hopi's will have theirs. The liberal colleges and universities have their set of truths, which will differ from the Christian conservative colleges. A home- schooling family will have their set of truths, which will vary from the public schooled child. The medical doctor has his set of truths, and the homeopathic has theirs.

A value of a truth can even reach down into our preference of pets. This breed is better than that breed. This food is the best. Raw vs: cooked. The cat lovers vs. the dog lovers. Those are all their perceived truths.

My grandparents' generation watched a wicked man, Hitler, twist his beliefs so greatly that they became truths to thousands of people. His propaganda then became a truth. We can see it again and again as evil men rise up and convince people of their truth.

But those are not really truths at all. They are opinions and beliefs and even preferences, lodged in our brains so deep and twisted that we identify them as truths.

There are only two absolutes on earth; gravity and death. And both are created by God Almighty. Conception is a truth only if it happens and that is not always a truth as some women may never conceive; but a woman can fall out of a tree and hit the ground (gravity) and all women will eventually pass away (death).

We have our laws, put together by men of the highly esteemed, but even those are not truths. We can murder and never get caught, by man. We can slander, steal, abuse, lie, cheat, covet, even curse The Father and

The Son; and never suffer the 'truth' punishment by man. So, these man laws are not truths, they are just what they are, laws.

But the genuine truths are those of The Father, those are the truths that will be the consequences of our actions.

There is only one truth in the universe, and that is The Father and what He creates. His Son is His truth. His Torah is His truth. The life we live through Him is truth.

Truth and faith can be synonyms in a world of complex ideas, technology and problems. If I trust in God and His Son, if I place my life in His Truth, I have just made the step towards unwavering faith. If I put my trust in the truths of man, my faith will waver greatly and even dissipate as I watch the world around me collapse.

"Show me your ways, O Elohim. Teach me your paths. Lead me in your truth and teach me." Psalms *Tehillim*, 25:4,5

"Send forth your light and your truth. Let them lead me." Psalms *Tehillim* 43:3

"Mercy and truth shall meet." Psalms *Tehillim* 85:10

Teach me your way O Elohim. Let me walk in your truth. Unite my heart to fear Your Name." Psalms *Tehillim* 86:11

"And guard the Charge of Elohim to walk in His Ways, to guard His laws, His commands, His right rulings and His witness as it is written in the Torah of Moses so that you do wisely all that you do and wherever you turn so that God does establish His Word which He spoke concerning me saying, 'If your sons guard their way to walk before me in truth with all their heart and with all their being, saying...." 1Kings *1Melakim* 2:4

Faith in Hebrew is *Emunah*, which can translate as steadfast. Faith is resolute in something, an idea or way of life or opinion. The key in the life that we live is to put our faith into the truth of the Father.

Recently, we attended a beautiful Seder in Denver at the Hyatt Regency,[1]. There were over seven hundred people there to praise The Father and The Son. Those people were believers in the entire truth, the Torah and Yeshua. It was a wonderful night. The next morning, the ballroom, just hours previously decorated with colors and signs for Yeshua The Messiah, was now decorated in pink and green with balloons everywhere and ice carvings of rabbits. Children were running every which way in search of eggs. It was Easter morning.

I have nothing against Easter, but is it a truth? One cannot live a lie while constantly exposed to the truth; so he will deny the validity of the truth, Rambam 3:11. [2]

If we look at life through our truth lenses we can perceive truth as we want it to be. But if we filter everything through the truth lenses of The Word, then truth will become an absolute.

In studying truth in Mussar, it was interesting to come across a disagreement between Shammai and Hillel regarding truth that people see and speak. They were disagreeing what to say to a bride. [3] Shammai's question was; do we praise her as is commanded in Jewish law that she is beautiful when she is not? Hillel's opinion was that we *do*. Shammai's belief was that we *don't*.

I think that both of these scholars have missed the mark. They are equating what is beautiful within their own boundaries, their own opinions, their own truths, and then forming a response to their reaction of her looks or physical features. Someone may prefer long hair, or no freckles, or no glasses, or a tall woman or slender or heavier…and the list can go on and on. These are personal preferences that we turn into truths to fit our ideals.

All brides are beautiful in the eyes of The Lord, even if at that time they are not in Torah or not walking with The Lord in their life. But, at that certain moment they are walking in a commandment, in a truth, even if they don't even realize it. *They are becoming a wife.*

We are not to judge their physical appearance at all. For to that groom, she is a beautiful bride! And the God that we serve does not make mistakes. We make the mistakes which cause the consequences in our lives.

Speaking the truth has to remain just that. We cannot mix our emotions or our preferences within those boundaries. If my child breaks a lamp and he is questioned, I expect the truth. These are facts, did you or did you not break the lamp. If he lies, he does so out of fear. Fear that he would get in trouble and punished. There is such a fine line regarding that scenario. But if I raise my son in the Truth of The Father and His Word, he will realize, with of course encouragement from his parents, that the truth far outweighs the lies that may be told for an instant.

Pirkei Avos teaches that one must be careful to speak the full truth, even regarding seemingly inconsequential details. Lying is habit forming; once ingrained it is almost impossible to eliminate from our system. Almost, inadvertently, we will continually slip into falsehood even when he has nothing to gain. Hillel taught that we are to love and pursue peace and that peace will only be effective if it is accompanied by justice and truth.

Torah is called the living Torah meaning that it must be translated into action. Since Torah is the blueprint of Creation, it contains the key to understanding God's Will even to the most seemingly mundane arenas of our daily movement. [4] Isn't that interesting that Torah is called the Living Torah. And the Holy Spirit brings it to life. Through that life, the Holy Spirit, we gain the truth. We can live by the truth.

This chapter, Truth is being written on the heels of Pesach, Passover. Our family as usual started the counting of the Omer and the reading of Psalms 119. If you have never read Psalms 119, I highly encourage you to read it as you work on the character trait of 'truth'. It is filled with God's Glory and what is His Truth.

"And they sent to Him their taught ones with the Herodians, saying, 'Teacher, we know that You are true and teach the way of Elohim in truth and it does not concern You about anyone for You are not partial about any man." Matthew *Mattithyahu* 22:16.

"And the Word became flesh and pitched His tent among us and we saw His esteem, esteem as of an only brought forth of The Father complete in favor and truth." John *Yohanan* 1:14.

"You worship what you do not know, we worship what we know, because the deliverance is of the Yehudim (Jews). *But the hour is coming and now is, when the true worshippers shall worship The Father in Spirit and Truth for The Father does also seek such to worship Him. Elohim is spirit and those who worship Him need to worship in Spirit and Truth."* John *Yohanan* 4:22-24.

John 14:6, 14:17, 17:17, Romans 2:13, Ephesians 6:14, 1Timothy 2:4, 2Timothy 3:8, 2Timothy 4:4.

"So Yeshua (Jesus) *said to those Yehudim* (Jews) *who believed Him, 'If you stay in My Word you are truly My taught ones. And you shall know the truth and the truth shall set you free."* John *Yohanan* 8:31,32.

"Your righteousness is righteousness forever. And Your Torah is truth." Psalms *Tehillim* 119:142.

"By this we know if we know Him if we guard His commands. The one who says, 'I know Him' and does not guard His commands is a liar and the truth is not in him." 1John 2:3. [4]

These Scripture verses tie in the Torah, The Father, The Son and His Word as Truth. If we have one without the other are we living in half-truths? If we live in a state of half-truths and preconceived truths that we have made true in our lives, we will be disconnected from the Source and live in chaos and in fear. The chaos and fear may or may not be apparent, but it will be in our lives.

Without truth there is fear. Fear is not the absence of the presence of God but the absence of direction. [5]

Fear is gripping and strangling. Fear is without direction and can be stagnating. But God has given us the emotion of fight or flight. That is an innate sense of power and discernment in a split second. Many of us have felt that feeling as it comes upon us without thinking, as The Spirit moves us out of danger or causes us to fight off the danger. People have spoken of extraordinary strength during times of fight or flight. Those reactions to a situation are not so much based on fear but wisdom given from The Father.

Hiking behind our house, our young boys came across a den of rattlesnakes. The boys were given a sense of calmness as they received the intuitive response of flight. They came home to Jay, who received the intuitive response of fight, that protective realm that a father gets for his child.

The fear that is gripping is man made. We convince ourselves of a fear. Fear of the unknown, fear of people, fear of germs, fear of the dark, fear of spiders, fear of dying, fear of dating, fear of heights, and fear of the ocean, etc.

A gripping fear came over me that Friday that the surgeon called to give me the results of the biopsy, malignant stage IIIB Breast Cancer. When I sat down and prayed, I realized that I was afraid because I knew nothing. I needed knowledge about the disease and treatments and I needed God's wisdom for the discernment of what I should do. That turned the disease into a truth; 'okay, so now I have breast cancer, it is in my DNA, my generational curses, and the consequences of when I was young.'

That knowledge also turned the treatments into a truth of what I would be going through and for how long. I spoke to other women and got information on line. I was no longer in a dark hole. There was reasoning.

God tells us in His Word to not be afraid of the events or life around us, which would be living a faithless life. We are to cast our fear to Him, which as we read in the beginning of this book, translates into *yirah* meaning awe/fear at the same time.

"After these events the word of YHWH came to Abram in a vision, saying, 'Do not be afraid, Abram, I am your shield, your reward is exceedingly great." Genesis *Bereshith,* 15:1

"Do not fear, for I am with you. Do not look around, for I am your Elohim. I shall strengthen you, I shall also help you, I shall also uphold you with the right hand of My righteousness." Isaiah *Yeshayahu* 41:10.

"Fear not for I am with you, I shall bring your seed from the east and gather you from the west." Isaiah *Yeshayahu* 43:5.

The fear of The Lord is the beginning of wisdom, Psalms 111:10. The fear of The Lord is to hate evil, Proverbs 8:13, but we are told to not fear evil, Psalms 23:4.

We are told that the midwives feared God, Exodus 1. We are told that the fear of The Lord is the fountain of life, Proverbs 14:27. We are told not to fear those that kill the body, Matthew 10:28. And in Revelation 2:10 we are told *"...do not be afraid of what you are about to suffer..."*

We are to fear The Lord, to be in awe and reverence of Him. That will gain knowledge and wisdom. We are not to fear evil around us- we are to be over comers. We are not to fear what can be done to the body, for we are given eternal life.

In the book of Judges, chapter 1 it is commanded three times to not fear and be of courage. In 1Chronicles 28:10 The Lord tells us to build a house, be strong and do it! Be victorious and courageous! Do not fear!

There is another reason for us to be afraid, for us to have fear. *"For he is God's minister to you for good. But if you do evil, be afraid..."* Hebrews 13:4a. If we do evil, we are to be afraid.

But we are commanded not to fear the evil around us, and to be strong and courageous. Isn't that interesting? The truth is to fear The Lord by gaining His knowledge, and to be afraid if *we* do evil. We are to be courageous and courageous is listed 98 times in Scripture. Have you read the end of the book? We win!

Rabbi Messer teaches that doubt is as powerful as faith; it will produce disasters as quickly as faith will produce miracles. To live in unwavering faith is to live in unwavering truth and to live in doubt is to live in fear. To live in faith and truth produces action since The Torah is an action, a verb. When we live in truth and faith we are really living in His faithfulness and in His truth.

We can speak fear into our lives and into the lives of others. Speak life into your life and into the lives of others. Draw a line between opinions and truth. Draw a line between preference and truths. What is propaganda, what is truth?

When my husband told Rabbi and Maureen Messer about the diagnosis of breast cancer, we were genuinely afraid. Afraid of the word itself, cancer; it carries such a stigma. We were afraid of the unknown. We knew nothing! And of course, you're well one moment, yet a doctor is telling you that cancer is lurking within your body. It's a very debilitating feeling. You're suddenly stuck in a time warp with fear gripping you at all sides. What is the truth? Am I going to die? Do I need surgery? Chemo? And on and on.

"Keep moving forward. Don't lose your focus. And beware of counterfeits." Those were the words of Rabbi Messer that Sunday when we told him the news.

Keep moving forward, don't lose your focus. Pray, pray for truth and wisdom. In *Everyday Holiness The Path of Mussar*, Alan Morinis quotes, "distance yourself from falsehood." And as the Alter of Novarodok teaches, we are easily confused about truth because truth can appear before us in the guise of falsehood just as falsehood can show up before us in the trappings of truth.[6]

The statement of beware of the counterfeit had us puzzled at first. Rabbi Messer gave no instruction, just that simple declarative sentence. But it wasn't long before falsehood (the counterfeit) came to us disguised in the trappings of truth, bringing doubt and fear. Truth is the area where lies are exposed and living in fear is allowing death to speak into your life.[7]

It was through prayer and His Word that brought us back to the truth that He had given us and once again we were moving forward and we had regained our focus.

In this day, there can be so much to be fearful of. And so much falsehood has become the truth. But our positions of ones who are covered by The Father and His Word are not to live in fear. Fear in and of itself of the right choices, is not a sinful emotion. Fear can become sinful when we fail to obey God *because* of our fears. And those fears can be as simple as being afraid to go against the majority.

Trust and faith are synonymous with truth. What is the Father's truth? What does He declare is false? What are we to fear? Rabbi Sha'ul (Paul) says that a man full of doubt is like one who looks in the mirror and forgets his own face. Fear and doubt are synonymous with falsehood. Lies will keep you gripped in fear. Have you ever told a lie to your parents as a young child? We were frozen in fear that they would find out we were lying! The truth has a release about it. It will set you free. That is what Jesus is speaking of when He says: the truth shall set you free. His truth, His ways! It frees us from man's bondage, from fear of man.

"I have hated doubting thoughts
But have loved Your Torah
You are my hiding place and my shield
I have waited for Your word
Turn away from me you evil doers

For I observe the commands of my Elohim!
Support me according to Your Words
That I might live
And put me not to shame
Because of my expectation
Sustain me that I might be saved
And always look to Your laws
You have made light of all those
Who stray from Your laws
For falsehood is in their deceit
You have made to cease
All the wrong of the earth like dross
Therefore I have loved Your witnesses
My flesh has trembled for fear of You
And I am in awe of Your right rulings"
Psalms *Tehillim* 119:113-120

How do you know if something is true? We have to look at 'it' objectively. The very problem is that when we do the looking, we are conditioned by the very thing we are looking at, which makes objectivity almost impossible.[8] When people view things from the guise of their own opinion, it will 'make them right in their own eyes'. No on ever sees themselves as others do (Pastor Jay Howard).

Hate is not a truth, it is taught. Children are not born into this world hating each other. [9] So, is hate the truth? Or is the lesson of hating the truth.

Our God is a God of loving-kindness, and forgiveness. The truth is that God's forgiveness is unconditional and timeless; we are already forgiven; Mark 2:5-12.

God's love is *ahavah rabbah*, infinite love which is unbounded, absolute, here, then, now and always. It is constant. If we are already loved and already forgiven, then the truth is to cultivate loving kindness through truth and forgiveness, of ourselves and others. Truth is that God is in control and to deny His part in the playing of our lives is to deny the truth that He put in motion everything that happens in this world. God is not circumstance or a wild card.

The paradox is that we must embrace the truth of not knowing.

1. Rabbi Ralph Messer, Simchat Torah Beit Midrash, Denver CO
2. Pirkei Avos, The Ethics of the Fathers
3. Everyday Holiness The Path of Mussar, Alan Morinis
4. Pirkei Avos, The Ethics of the Fathers
5. Rabbi Ralph Messer, Simchat Torah Beit Midrash Denver CO
6. Everyday Holiness The Path of Mussar, Alan Morinis
7. Pastor Jay Howard, Simchat haMashiach Beit Emunah
8. The Sacred Art of Loving Kindness Preparing to Practice, Rabbi Rami Shapiro
9. The Sacred Art of Loving Kindness Preparing to Practice, Rabbi Rami Shapiro

Vickie Howard

<u>Notes</u>　　　　　　<u>Week Five</u>　　　　　　<u>Truth</u>

Code word or words:

Situations to recognize:

Truth

Day One:

Day Two:

Day Three:

Day Four:

Day Five:

Day Six:

Day Seven:

The Exercise:

This exercise takes time and thinking, and honesty. If you were to write down all the times that you were offended at someone or something, what would you see? In an offense, so many times we think we heard something, or we react to an episode that we have made into a truth.

On a piece of paper, maybe in your journal, make two columns, one titled truth and one titled false.

You can start with your physic, or your soul traits or your intellect. What is true about me? Did she really say that I was fat? Or is it that she said nothing after I had lost 10 pounds and I took it as 'oh, she thinks I'm fat'. What am I classifying as truth?

Or, you can start with God's word. What is true? What is false? One classic example is in the book of Acts. In Acts 12:4 most translations read: *"So when he had arrested him, he put him in prison and delivered him to four squads of soldiers to keep him intending to bring him before the people after Easter."*

Easter? Easter is not a truth in God's word. It is in truth *Passover*. The resurrection of Yeshua/ Jesus, 3 days after His death and burial is an absolute, a truth. But Easter is not a God truth. It is a man's holiday that coincides with the sun, and became the day that is recognized as resurrection Sunday.

I am not trying to start a theological debate; I am simply trying to show how easy an idea can become a truth in our minds.

For this exercise you will have to be honest with yourself. Take everything you know and put it on a shelf and ask God to mercifully show you His Truths. He will. Be humble in the truths that you are shown.

Now, for the character trait of fear, again make two columns: one truth and one false. What is it you fear? Is it a truth or a lie? Chemotherapy is a truth. But what did I fear? Vomiting? Yes, that's a truth. Feeling horrible? Yes, that's a truth. Losing my hair? Another truth. Losing my fingernails? Truth. Damaging my heart? (I had Adriomyacin). Another truth. Dying? Probably a lie. Some well-intentioned people told me I would be killing myself if I took chemotherapy. But, that is where The Father was leading me. So, I could combat these fears with knowledge. By listing the fears, I could see what I needed to battle and what I could let go of. Remember: a half- truth is a whole lie.

List everything, write them down. Once on paper you will be able to actually see what it is that you fear. Is it God? Is it *yirah* (fear/awe) of The Father, or is it something that we have placed in our very soul? Trust in Him, He won't let you go.

You can do this.

Be strong and courageous do not fear nor be afraid of them. For it is YHWH your Elohim who is going with you, He does not fail nor forsake you. Deuteronomy 31:6

Silence

Death and life are in the power of the tongue.

Proverbs *Mishle* 18:21

Silence, *sh'tikah* in Hebrew.
Speak life.
A word rightly spoken.
Silence is golden.
Speech is the mirror of the heart.
Out of the abundance of the mouth, the heart does speak.
"So then, my beloved brothers, let every man be swift to hear, slow to speak and slow to wrath. James *Ya'aqob* 1:19

You learn more by listening; for you already know what you would say.

People who talk about themselves seldom want to hear what others would say.

There is no better medicine than silence.

Silence helps us to hear the voice of God.

In 1Kings we are told that there was an earthquake, a fire, wind and storm yet God was not in these. Then, after was a still small voice. (In Hebrew it is literally 'a soft gentle rustling').

To listen one has to be silent. To understand what someone is really trying to say, one has to be quiet and hear.

We have become so accustomed to noise that there is almost an embedded narrow-mindedness against the idea that silence just may be beneficial. If you tell someone to be quiet, they may sneer at you like a crabby old man. But it has never been more essential in this world today to carve out a little bit of silence.

"Shema Israel, Adonai Eloheynu Adonai Echad." Deuteronomy *Debarim* 6:4. Hear O Israel, The Lord is God The Lord is One.

In Deuteronomy 6:4 YHWH is telling His people to hear. We can't hear if we aren't quiet and listen. The sound of silence is eternity.[1]

The attributes of silence go beyond listening. We can pretend to listen but our mind is racing. We can listen but not really hear what the person is saying. We can listen and interject our emotions so that we hear what we want to hear. Silence concerns our speech, also. What words we choose to say and how we say them. Silence is about our tone, our body movements and posture. Often times what we say in silence is more than if we were to use words.

The teacher of the Alter of Novarodok, Rabbi Yisrael Salanter, made silence the final of the thirteen soul traits that he listed on his Mussar practice curriculum. What he said about silence and what mostly is taught in Mussar practice is the restraint in speech.[2] Restraint in speech is a learned character trait. I don't think there isn't a two year old in the world that doesn't shout 'mine!' when they want a toy.

We can use our silence and our speech to edify or rebuke or demolish. I can be quiet, but with just a look of the eyes, my boys know they are in trouble. I can choose my words carefully and edify my husband with my speech and my tone, or I can give him the silent treatment and hurt his feelings. Silence can easily become an idol of the heart, so we must be wise too, in our silence.

I can shout back at my husband or I can be silent and let him vent. Silence, speech and body language, can be intertwined into one.

Silence isn't edifying if it is meant to hurt. Speech and words should always be chosen with wisdom. In silence there is wisdom, for you will hear and learn. In silence you won't speak.

The primary guideline in Mussar for speech is not whether something is true or not but rather what impact our words will have.[3] If in our speech we may cause any type of harm, we are to seize our tongues. Just because I don't like the dress doesn't mean it is a truth.

In *Pirkei Avos*, it is written that silence is the protective fence for wisdom. However, wisdom itself is the ability to not necessarily remain totally silent but to be in control of one's speech so that he may engage appropriately in discussion.

"All my days I have been raised among the Sages and I found nothing better for oneself than silence."[4]

Shamon in *Pirkei Avos* writes that his life experience among wise men has taught him that one who remains silent at least *appears* to be intelligent; if he is quick to respond to people rather than silently hearing them out, he is bound to speak foolishly (Rashi).

Rambam categorizes five types of speech:

1. Mitzvah – speech involving the Torah, study, reading, and prayer.
2. Forbidden – false testimony, falsehood, gossip, cursing, and gossip.
3. Tasteless – idol talk, gossip.
4. Worthwhile – praising intelligent or virtuous character.
5. Permissible – business and domestic issues.
6. *Lashon hara*, in Hebrew literally means evil tongue and *sh'mirat ha'lashon* means guarding the tongue. Gossip, slander and falsehood fall into this category.

The Ba'al Shem Tov, founder of the eighteenth century Jewish movement called Chasidism (from the Hebrew word *chesed*, meaning kindness) taught that each of us is born with a fixed number of words to speak, and when we have spoken the last of these we die.[5] Would our everyday speech change if this was/is the truth? What does our Messiah in truth mean when He says: *"And I say to you that for every idle word men speak, they shall give an account of it in the Day of Judgment"* (deliverance). Matthew *Mattithayahu* 12:36.

The Chofetz Chaim is famous for his caution regarding all areas of speech. Mussar teaches that there are four main types of negative speech. The first type would be degrading statements spoken about a person or persons that in fact are actually true. "She's an awful cook" may be a true sentence in our minds, but by saying that, we damage her cooking reputation to someone who might otherwise love her cooking. (This negative speech does not include the absolute truth/facts that are about a dangerous person, meant as a safety warning).

The second type of speech would be when the negative statements that are being spread are false. The third type of speech would be spreading negative speech that we may have 'heard'. "I heard she was an awful cook."

The fourth type of negative speech would be to imply a negative thought about someone. "Boy, you'd think she would be a better cook considering how old she is."

I have found that practicing silence and speech in Mussar is really two fold.

The first stage would be to work on silence. There are specific areas in The Scriptures when silence is best and unconditional. *"A time to rend and a time to sew; a time to keep silence and a time to speak."* Ecclesiastics

Qoheeth 3:7. "*But the Lord is in His holy temple, let all the earth keep silence before Him.*" Habakkuk *Habaqquq* 2:20.

Rabbi Israel Salanter, founder of Mussar focused on virtue and taught that the key to righteous living is to say what you mean and do what you say. Rabbi Shapiro tells us that this is not as easy as it may sound. For saying what we mean and then regarding what we are exactly saying requires us to be lucid about what is happening (truth) and to respond to it from a spacious mind rather than a narrow mind.[6]

Every person and every body needs silence. We need silence to pray, to sleep, to read, to think, to listen and to hear. *"Hush all flesh, before YHWH for He has roused Himself out of His set apart dwelling!"* Zechariah *Zekaryah* 2:13. *"And when He opened the seventh seal there came to be silence in the heaven for about half an hour."* Revelation 8:1.

There are a few exercises you can do to strengthen the soul trait of silence.

First thing you should try and accomplish is when you arise in the morning; give yourself a few moments of silence. Go into a quiet space and pray. Implement that behavior before you sleep, give yourself another few moments of silence, deep breathing and prayer. If you have a TV in the bedroom, try to leave it off once you get in bed. Enjoy the silence and listen to God.

Another exercise you can do is when someone, anyone, everyone is speaking to you, make a conscious effort to be still and listen. Stop whatever you are doing (are we really multi tasking or are we just being busy in a lot of areas?) and grab a hold of what they are saying. Look at their eyes, observe the body language and do not react with words until they are done with what they are saying. I have had to even tell myself to stop! – And listen.

I have found that when my children are trying to tell me something and I keep going in my 'busy-ness' I really don't hear what they are saying, and then later on in the day, that old maxim will come up: 'but you said!' Also, I have taken into practice that when I am speaking to my children, it makes a world of difference when I make them stop and look at me in the eyes and listen.

One of the hardest points of silence is to be quiet while we are being accused. This is a learned behavior, for the flesh desires to defend itself, to lash out at our accusers. In regards to this, we pray that God gives us the grace and strength that our Savior had so many times. Matthew 26:62, 63; Matthew 27:14 and Luke 23:9.

How can an argument ensue if half of the whole is quiet? Our perfect example is Yeshua who was quiet when they brought the accused woman to him. John *Yohanan* 8:6.

Another exercise in regards to silence is the negative aspect of it. Silence can be a wall that divides people, congregations, family, and friends. If you have an opportunity to break a silence, do so with encouraging, or apologetic words. How many times have we heard someone say: "oh, she hasn't spoken to her mother/father/sister/whatever, in years." What does it matter in the heavens if you were right and they were wrong?

"Pleasant words are as a honeycomb, sweet to the soul and health to the bones." Proverbs *Mishle* 16:24.

Another silence that can kill is between husband and wife. It can build a wall so thick it will almost be, if not, impenetrable. 'Honey, I'm sorry, I love you.' What magic words!

Once you have identified the appropriate areas in your life for silence and speaking, the essence of speech comes into play.

Words can bring life or they can kill. There are hurtful words, gossip words and negative words. One of the hardest areas in life is controlling the tongue. But it *can* be accomplished. It just takes a moment of time, allow yourself time to process what the other person is saying. Then, allow yourself a moment in time to rightly answer that person. Sometimes you don't need to or can't answer. At that point, a smile is best.

"Let your word always be with favor, seasoned with salt, so that you know how you ought to answer each one." Colossians 4:6.

"For we all stumble in many matters. If anyone does not stumble in word, he is a perfect man, able to also bridle the entire body." James *Ya'aqob* 3:2 (read all of James 3).

"For he who wishes to love life and see good days, let him keep his tongue from evil and his lips from speaking deceit, let him turn away from evil and do good, let him seek peace and pursue it." 1Peter *Kepha* 3:10, 11. Notice how this Scripture ties in peace with speaking good things not evil. When I say things to my husband that I should not say: I feel horrible. I definitely do not have peace. I can't sleep! But as soon as I correct my speech, it feels like a thousand pounds have been lifted off of me.

The guidance of Mussar teaches that there is a two-step practice in working on any soul trait. The first stage of practice involves developing sensitivity, learning to be aware to the silence and speech around you and within you. The second stage is restraint. The new attentiveness in our lives of each of these character traits now calls out for active steps to change the circumstances of our lives.[7]

Think about these words: arrogance, conceit, egotism, haughtiness, being over confident and self-importance. Now put these words into a situation when someone talks about themselves. Have you ever been around a dinner table or at a party and there is a certain person that is going on and on about him/herself and no one else can speak? That is the character trait of a 'topper'. Someone tells a story of how they broke their leg and the 'topper' is quick to top that story. 'Oh, they broke both legs – twice!' Pastor Jay Howard from Colorado teaches that this falls under the nature of competitive conversation. People tend to think that competition is only in the physical realm, but it is very apparent in the linguistic and spiritual realm, too. The best thing to do is to walk away from competitive conversation, for the results go nowhere. There will be a loser and a winner. And most of the time the winner is the one that is either louder or more aggressive, which has nothing to do with living in the Kingdom of God.

To demand to be the center stage of a conversation, whether it is between people or God, is an arrogant attitude that they are better deserved of that space and time to speak. It is a self-important position that allows that person to fulfill his/her needs by possessing someone else's moment that is given by YHWH.

The reasons that the arrogant person hardly ever listens is due to the fact that he/she is self seeking and really does not see how anything the other person has to say could benefit him/her. He/she is in this world for themselves and all quality and quantity of life revolves around them.

To gossip about someone is also the character trait of an arrogant person, for in fact gossip usually revolves around what the person conceives as 'sin' in that other person's life. They can also be comparing themselves with the person they are gossiping about and in that way are self-edifying. It is a self-seeking motive, for gossip tends to tear down a person in order to up another person in the eyes of man.

There is another reason for the *la'shon ha'rah*; whatever that person is gossiping about, could possibly be in their lives. The Father has a way of bringing things out in the open in very unusual ways. Things will manifest.

Rabbi Yitzchok Ruderman teaches us to appreciate human speech as no less a miracle than speech to a donkey. We should never take our speech for granted, and regard our every utterance as a renewal of the Almighty's blessing of communication.[8]

So out of our mouths, may there flow blessings not curses. May we speak life and not death. May we build up and not tear down. May we cultivate loving kindness and not bitterness. May we glorify The Father in our speech.

1. Pastor Jay Howard Simchat haMashiach Beit Emunah
2. Everyday Holiness, The Path of Mussar, Alan Morinis
3. Everyday Holiness, The Path of Mussar, Alan Morinis
4. Pirkei Avos, The Ethics of the Fathers
5. The Sacred Art of Loving Kindness Preparing to Practice, Rabbi Rami Shapiro
6. The Sacred Art of Loving Kindness Preparing to Practice, Rabbi Rami Shapiro
7. Everyday holiness, The Path of Mussar, Alan Morinis
8. Pirkei Avos, The Ethics of the Fathers, Mesorah Publications

Vickie Howard

<u>*Notes*</u>　　　　<u>*Week Six*</u>　　　　<u>*Silence*</u>

Code word or words:

Situations to recognize:

Silence

Day One:

Day Two:

Day Three:

Day Four:

Day Five:

Day Six:

Day Seven:

The Exercise:

Carry something in your pocket or purse or in your hand. A rubber band, a thumbtack, a paperclip, a pecan, anything. When you are engaging in conversation, either on the speaking end or listening side, grab that item, unbeknownst to the other party, and concentrate on it. You are now causing yourself to think of a distraction, which in turn will help you concentrate on what the person is saying and what you should *not* say or say or not hear or hear.

Listen, listen, listen and roll that rubber band around in your fingertips, and think of listening. Is what I am about to say worth it? Is it edifying? Is what I am about to hear is it worth it? Is it edifying?

Pastor Jay Howard teaches that you never see yourself as others see you. That is a scary statement, because most of us see ourselves as pretty darn good.

If you run a conversation, and you will have to be honest with yourself to see if you do; then be quiet. "That which you see and hear, you can not help; but that which you say depends on you alone." -Zohar

Get that rubber band out, or play with that tack in your pocket and every time you want to say something, poke yourself, or rub that rubber band over those delicate little hairs on your fingers. Ask questions instead of telling. Talk *with* the person instead of *at* them. Seek the answer not the problem.

"A wise man's question contains half the answer." –Soloman Ibn Gabirol.

You can do this, too!

Yeshua stood up and commanded the wind and said to the waves, "Quiet! Be still!" Then the wind stopped and it became completely calm. Mark 4:39

Humility

The reward of humility is the yirah of YHWH. Proverbs 22:4

Humility is a character trait that Yeshua lived and taught; yet He taught humility with strength. Rabbi Messer teaches that humility is strength under control and Pastor Jay Howard tells us that humility is a state of mind where peace is found.

In the book of Genesis, God created Adam from *Adamah*, the earthling from the earth. Adam was not originally a person's name, but the name of a species: humanity from humus, earth. The word humility comes from the same Latin root; to be humble is to return to the original nature or original status as in the image and likeness of God. That is, let God manifest you in your time and place as His likeness.[1]

Like any character trait, humility can become the obsession or the idol itself. A person can become so humble, in their dress, their actions, their state of mind, that actually there is a self- indulgence in oneself in their humility.

True humility is linked with honor, in that the very presence of humility is that we are going to give honor to someone over us. Humility is not about us – but about others. Humility is honoring the God that made us and knowing that He also made the person to our right and to our left. To honor His people is honoring our King in humility.

Olelos Ephraim notes that because of his humility, Moses showed no reluctance to accept the Torah at Sinai, as he had when God assigned him the mission to deliver the Hebrew people from their Egyptian bondage. There, Moses had expressed uncertainties about whether he was the proper man for the task. In this case, however, taking his signal from Sinai, which by the way is the lowest and symbolically most humble of all mountains, Moses was sure that he was the proper person for the job.[2]

In his book, Alan Morinis [3], instructs us that in traditional Jewish understanding, humility has nothing to do with being the lowest, most debased, shrinking creature on earth. Rabbi Abraham Isaac Kook who was the first Ashkenazi Chief Rabbi of Israel said that humility is associated with spiritual perfection. When humility causes depression it is defective, and when it is genuine it inspires joy, courage and inner dignity. The

Messiah is the second half of that previous sentence. He had genuine humility, which inspired and *inspires* us in joy, courage and dignity. Rabbi Sha'ul, Paul, tells us that we are given a spirit of courage, not a spirit of self debasement.

Mussar teaches that humility and self esteem go hand in hand. Which leads up to the fact that there are four levels in regards to humility. They begin at self-debasement, continue to humility, then pride and finish at arrogance. At both ends of the range; self-debasement and arrogance, is the word 'I'. Both of these character traits swallow up space around them as the person becomes completely focused on themselves in an unhealthy and unrealistic way. In both traits we see ourselves first and before anyone, either as a mini god; which is one side of the spectrum; or a wretched person that shouldn't be alive, which is the other side of the range. Both traits are extreme areas of idolatry and both are unholy attributes, for both soul traits take up more space and more of us. Again, me, me, me.

Humility is not about us. It is not about how humble I can be in my dress, my demeanor, and my actions. For if that is the case, I am actually not humble at all but again, focused on my self.

"It is not good to eat much honey, is it esteem to seek ones own esteem?" Proverbs *Mishle* 25:27.

Yet, humility is about speech, too. In joining in on a conversation, is it really necessary that I say something? Is the point I am about to make to the benefit and edifying of others around me?

There is a teaching in Mussar; no more than my place no less than my space. God has given each human a soul, a holy soul. We are not the creators of our souls or someone else's soul. God has given each person the right to live and make choices as he lives. We are in free will, constantly. We are not the judge, or the holy soul counter. We can not see the future, nor should we wallow in the past. God tells us that each one in his own life is responsible for their relationship with Him and to be humble before Him. *"And my people upon whom My Name is called shall humble themselves and pray and seek My Face and turn from their evil ways then I shall hear from the heavens and forgive their sin and heal their land."* 2Dibre haYamim 2Chronicles 7:14.

Even King Ahab at a certain point knew to humble himself before The Lord. 1Kings, *1Melakim* 21:29.

Entering into a crowded elevator, you have the human need to have some space on that elevator. If it is getting crowded, you move into the corner, but you don't recoil into a corner and yet you don't stand in the middle of the elevator expecting others to move around you or for them to cringe into a corner. No more than my place no less than my space.

Our Messiah gives us the perfect example of humility, that which comes in a child. *"Whoever then humbles himself as this little child is the greatest in the reigns in the heavens."* Matthew *Mattithayhu* 18:4

God endows man with a living soul and invests him with many abilities and talents but it is all on loan, to be wisely reinvested on God's behalf and eventually returned to Him. Humility does not mean being ignorant to one's unique capabilities; it is the acknowledgment that one's uniqueness is on loan and that such a loan cannot be a source of personal pride.[4]

We can be conscious of our talents, and yet be humbly aware that they are no cause for pride. Such a person knows that all his abilities are on loan, to be used appropriately during this lifetime. For even time is on loan from God. Moses knew that God spoke to him directly, yet he was the most humble of all men. (Numbers *Bemidbar* 12:3).

In the soul trait humility, we are putting our trust in The Father; we all know that nothing we have is due to ourselves, our power or our self esteem. In our honoring of others, we actually become honored. Who is honored? He who honors.

Humility is about honor. *Kavod* is honor in Hebrew and means to honor others, to help others, to pray for others is to honor The King. If you honor another, you are expressing humility without saying it.

In Daniel 2:30, Daniel tells the King that the secret was not revealed to him because he had more wisdom than anyone living. He gave the glory to God, which led to him promotion.

Moses in Exodus 3:1-12 recognizes his limitations and Gods' holiness. Solomon in 1Kings 3:11 understood his boundaries and didn't seek his own glory, which led to riches and honor. The Centurion in Matthew 8:5-10 knew of his unworthiness and that led to God's grace and mercy in his life. When Joseph was enslaved and imprisoned, he gave God the glory and in turn he was honored and given great authority. Genesis 41:14-44.

"But the meek ones shall inherit the earth and delight themselves in plenty of peace". Psalms *Tehillim* 37:11.

Humility is like a beautiful rose with its splendor, its fragrance and the colors. It is one of the most striking flowers. We can encourage those around us to love the Savior and seek His grace and mercy when and only when we are humble in our speech, walk, attitude, body language and in our honest listening. Matthew 5:16. When we become that rose.

In Simchat haMashiach Beit Emunah, Pastor Jay Howard honors the elders by listening, learning from and expecting the younger members to assist them. We are humbled merely by their experiences in life, and we encourage the thirty and twenty- something's to seek the wisdom of the older generation. It is probably true that these twenty and thirty something's could out tech, out maneuver, out talk, out read and out hear our older generations, but is that the point? Is that the truth?

The act of humility has many fingers. In a congregation, there are those people that desire the mic, those that want the stage, the glory of teaching, to be seen and to be heard. But can one humble themselves first, by volunteering to work in the nursery, or teach the young children. That is a test of humility. Can we sing our songs in a nursing home before we sing on stage? Can we rub the feet of the elderly before we get our pedicures? Can we love the unlovable?

Humility can encase pride, which is likened to a chain. "*So pride is their chain. The garment of violence covers them. Their eyes bulge from fatness, their heart overflows with imaginations.*" Psalms *Tehillim* 73:6.

So, humility without honor of others can develop pride.

Psalms 119:69, 70 says that pride is as fat as grease and pride is as a high wall in Proverbs 18:11.

The prideful person always sees themselves right in their own eyes. This will cause us to be proud in many of the soul traits. Anger is proud. Why am I angry? Because I think I'm right. Arguing is a spin of a prideful heart. Why are we arguing? To win, of course. We certainly don't argue to lose the debate. Impatience is riddled with pride. Why are we impatient with that person/driver/computer/child? Because *our* time is being wasted. Why are we bored with that Rabbi/Pastor/Elder? Because our knowledge is greater, we have pride in *our* understanding of the Scriptures.

In Numbers 16, *Qorah, Dathan* and *Abiram* rose up before Moses and they exalted themselves. They were argumentative and were causing a division in the camp. There was a spirit of jealousy and rebellion, which led to pride, which led to their deaths. This was the Jezebel influence. Pride will kill us, spiritually, if not physically, too. Our pride can develop into bitter root judgments because we will see ourselves better than someone and will hold that bitter root in us until we are exalted and then even if we are exalted above that person bitter root will remain for our pride will reach out and snag another area. There, then, the enemy has mastered us in our humility which went into pride which landed into bitterroot. Haman is a perfect example of this.

If you struggle with pride, take a moment and breathe, yes breathe. Go back to situations that you may have tried to out do someone, in speech, looks, and knowledge, your walk in Torah, your relationship with Yeshua, whatever. Ask yourself why? What does it matter – in the end – if you are better/faster/quicker/smoother?

Do you need encouragement? Do you need stroking? Are you lacking in forgiving yourself? Turn the pride around and honor that person.

YHWH is the source that we must cling to. When we elevate ourselves above and beyond our counterparts, we remove Him from being our source and we become our own source.

"He has declared to you O man, what is good. And what does YHWH require of you but to do right and to love kindness, and to walk humbly with your Elohim?" Mikah 6:8

There is a great story of a Rabbi who pointed a woman back to the source.

A woman came to a Rabbi begging for him to bless her so that she might conceive and have a child. He told her he could not and for her to leave. She was despondent and begged him to bless her. Again, he told her he could not and for her to leave. She left the Rabbi more upset than when she had entered. Soon, the Rabbi told his assistant to fetch her and bring her back. She came back into the office of the Rabbi, visually upset.

"When you first came in here, what did you think?" The Rabbi asked her.

"I knew that you are a holy man, and I wanted your blessing so that I may have a child." She answered.

"And what did you think when I sent you away?" He asked.

"Well, if you weren't going to bless me I have no resort but to turn to God." She answered.

"And what did you do?" He asked.

"I turned to God." She replied.

The Rabbi pointed her to The Source.

Pride will kill us. Proverbs *Mishle'* 16:18.

Humility with honor will cause us to advance. Proverbs *Mishle'* 22:4, Isaiah *Yeshayahu* 29:19:

"And the meek ones shall increase their joy in YHWH...."

1. The Sacred Art of Loving Kindness Preparing to Practice, Rabbi Rami Shapiro
2. Everyday Holiness, The Path of Mussar, Alan Morinis
3. Everyday Holiness, The Path of Mussar, Alan Morinis
4. Pirkei Avos, The Ethics of The Fathers, Mesorah Publications

Notes Week Seven Humility

Code word or words:

Situations to recognize:

Humility

Day One:

Day Two:

Day Three:

Day Four:

Day Five:

Day Six:

Day Seven:

The Exercise:

"*He has shown you O man, what is good; And what does the Lord require of you, but to do justly, to love mercy and to walk humbly with your God.*" Micah 6:8

That verse tells us that we are walking with God, not against Him. Everything we are, everything we have is because of Him. Nothing we do is the gift of ourselves, to ourselves, or because of ourselves.

Each morning as your feet hit the floor; thank God that you are alive. You could be dead, right? Realize that the beat in your heart is because of Him. That simple act of acknowledging Him before you start your day will put you in an awareness of life.

Now, when you take your time of quietness to offer praise to Him, thank Him for someone that you may have an 'issue' with. Thank Him for someone that maybe has bitterroot against you. Ask The Father to Bless that person.

Humility comes from the fear of the knowledge of the wisdom of The Lord. That's pretty simple.

Let someone cut in front of you. Each day as you work on this trait, allow someone to go ahead of you, or go first, or have the better seat or the best piece of cake at the potluck. Let some one be right in a conversation. Let some speak first and last. Let God direct your heart and your words.

Humility and honor. Humility is ours, honor is God's.

You can do this. Go to the source, and give honor to Him.

If you want to make peace you don't talk to your friends, you talk to your enemies.
Moshe Dayan.

Loving-kindness

The purpose of the Torah is to promote compassion, loving-kindness and peace in the world. Moses Maimonides

I chose loving-kindness to be the last chapter in this section because it is the defining character trait. If one develops loving- kindness to the degree that our Messiah desires us to have, then other negative soul traits will diminish.

In *Everyday Holiness, The Path of Mussar*, Alan Morinis talks about three levels of loving-kindness. Some will equate it with being nice. Others equate it with the Hebrew word *Chesed* which is to have mercy and grace. If you are nice to someone it is a totally different concept than if you have *chesed*, mercy or grace on someone. God sustains us with His mercy, His grace, His *chesed*, and His loving-kindness; not because He is nice.

God is the mercy and grace that upholds us. That is why we are told to worship Him in Spirit and in Truth. His Truth is the *chesed* that we are given. God is not a being or even a supreme being. He is being itself. [1]

Rabbi Shapiro teaches that grace is to life as current is to ocean. Grace is the dynamic nature of things, the flow, the dance the turning of the universe. In Isaiah, *Yeshayahu* 16:5 we are told that God's throne is founded in grace. [2]

Mussar teaches that action is the fundamental key to opening the heart. In a previous chapter I wrote of a Rabbi telling us that our hearts are closed and that we must circumcise our hearts before we can feel loving – kindness.

In an action we can show *chesed* upon others. Alan Morinis gives a great account of loving kindness as an action. If you are walking and see someone with a heavy box, you may jump in and help carry it. But, if you are walking the opposite way, and you stop and then help carry the box that is *chesed* in action. [3]

Judaism teaches that there are thirteen attributes of loving-kindness. This conclusion is drawn on the Scripture in Exodus, *Shemoth* 33:18, 19. God tells Moses that He will make all His goodness pass before him, calling out the goodness in turn: realizing the divinity of self, realizing the divinity of others, cultivating creativity, engendering compassion, finding grace, acting with equanimity, creating kindness, bringing forth truth, preserving kindness, forgiving iniquity, forgiving willfulness, forgiving error, and cleansing yourself of delusion. These are called the Thirteen Attributes of Loving-kindness.

Our Messiah is the pattern to loving-kindness, and is a mirror image of The Father. And we are made in the image and likeness of that pattern. Therefore we are in loving-kindness. Through The Lord we can abound in that agape love. The image is done; it's the likeness we have to work on. We again, are given the choice, the free will of our flesh. We can or we can not be in the image.

"By this shall all know that you are My taught ones, if you have love for one another." John, *Yohanan 13:35*.

"And the Master makes you increase and overflow in love to each other and to all, as we also do to you to establish your hearts blameless in set apartness before our Elohim and Father at the coming of our Master Yeshua Messiah with all His set apart ones!" 1Thessalonians 3:12.

"But the fruit of the Spirit is love, joy, peace, patience, kindness, goodness, trustworthiness, gentleness, self control. Against such there is no law." Galatians 5:22. God is The Spirit, the *chesed* and we thus we have to worship Him in Spirit and in Truth.

We can cultivate loving kindness in many ways. Through our speech, our generosity, our compassion, our empathy, our actions, our responses to actions, our reactions to emotions with in us, and our forgiveness.

There are two constant blocks to loving-kindness, either giving it or receiving it. They are anger and unforgiveness.

Anger keeps us from opening the door to wisdom by keeping us locked in the tiny space of narrow mind that will justify anger by insisting that we are the target. [4] Anger requires that we consider ourselves a target. It's a 'they are out to get me', attitude. It is a way for us to keep ourselves as the center of the story, and that becomes addictive for we remain the target, and self pity and self promotion consumes us. We maintain in a passive/aggressive mode – a victim-hood mentality.

Of course there is righteous anger, but for this topic we are not talking about the anger one would feel if a child was being hurt, or an animal. This anger is self promoted and is totally consumed by self. Anger is dangerous and deadly and will keep anyone from loving-kindness. The source is hasatan, which will keep you locked in bitterness and you will fail spiritually.

Future

You don't decide your future, you decide your habits and your habits decide your future. [5] Habits are created from determined action. Making it a habit to speak gently to people at all times will be a conscious action and will protect you from anger. Anger clouds our judgment and leaves us to make heinous errors.

Rabbi Shapiro teaches that loving-kindness doesn't just happen; it is a conscious effort, a purposeful habit that we must cultivate. It is an action.[6]

Unforgiveness is the second barrier that will keep us from receiving and showing loving-kindness. Unforgiveness creates bitter root judgment and that attacks the very soul of the very being of our existence. Often times, the spirit of bitter root judgment will birth revenge and vindictiveness in our character. That spirit is called the spirit of Jezebel or the Jezebel influence; 1Kings 19:2. Other examples are Ahab toward Micaiah, Haman toward the Jewish people, the Philistines toward Israel, and Herodias toward John the Immerser (Baptist). Bitterroot will make you vindictive (Genesis 21:10) instead of forgiving and loving.

"Do not take vengeance or bear a grudge against the children of your people. And you shall love your neighbor as yourself. I am YHWH." Leviticus *Wayyiqra 19:18*

Bitter root judgment will cloud our thoughts and bring the great *self* of our lives into action. The stories will be the same: 'I'm offended' 'they did that to me' or 'I'm hurt'.

When you forgive a person of their actions, you become the beneficiary of that action, of the forgiveness. Your health will improve, your joy will come back and you will be able to show true and unconditional loving-kindness again.

The act of loving-kindness is man separating himself from the animal instinct nature, and bitter root will keep you locked into that animalistic nature. Holding grudges and harboring ill feelings and anger creates ones' own self harbor where ships of peace and goodness do not move. The waters will lay stagnant. [7]

Our Father is one of mercy, *chesed,* grace, kindness and long suffering. He has placed those qualities in each of us; it is our free will to nurture them or let them die. If we do not do what God has placed in our hearts, (not us but God) we will eventually do what hasatan has planted in our flesh. [8]

Loving-kindness is an art, a graceful way of expression. You can create this character trait with speech, generosity, forgiveness, body language, deeds and prayer. After all, doesn't loving – kindness really mean to love kindness. It doesn't matter if someone is kind to you. Our job is to rise above it all and be kind to them. To love kindness! Begin by *loving* the kindness that we can show to others. Is it joyful and peaceful to yell at some one, or to hate them? No, your blood pressure rises, the veins on your neck pop out, your stomach aches, and you hurt. It is truly joyful to be calm and kind to someone.

What type of pleasure do you get by letting someone in line at the market go ahead of you if they have 4 items and you have 100? A lot of pleasure, right? Expound on that in everyday life. Remember the joy that you felt. Bring that kindness in to all facets of your life.

The key to true loving- kindness is to cling to The Source, God. As we imitate Gods great traits in our own lives, through the grace of His Son, Yeshua, we become immune to the harshness around us, and bask in His loving – kindness, which allows us to give it full in return.

It's not easy. It's hard to love a cactus. [9] So how *do you* admire a cactus? From far away – but still we admire them.

We have small cacti growing in the back area of our house. Every summer they grow beautiful yellow succulent flowers. This past summer, my nine year old picked a flower and brought it to me. I asked him if he didn't get any stickers in his hand? At that very sentence, you could just see the wheels turning in his head. He dropped the flower and hollered ' Yes!' As if he hadn't thought of it before. He had all these fine little stickers in his fingers and hand which took some diligence and time getting them all out.

So how do you admire those flowers? From afar, just looking at their beauty, their different kind of beauty. And by not touching! How do you love a cactus? From afar.

1. Everyday Holiness, The Path of Mussar, Alan Morinis
2. The Sacred Art of Loving Kindness Preparing to Practice, Rabbi Rami Shapiro
3. Everyday Holiness, The Path of Mussar, Alan Morinis
4. The Sacred Art of Loving Kindness Preparing to Practice, Rabbi Rami Shapiro
5. Rabbi Ralph Messer, Simchat Torah Beit Midrash, Denver CO.
6. The Sacred Art of Loving Kindness Preparing to Practice, Rabbi Rami Shapiro
7. ibid
8. Rabbi Ralph Messer, Simchat Torah Beit Midrash, Denver, CO
9. Pastor Jay Howard, Simchat haMashiach Beit Emunah, Bayfield, CO

Notes _Week Eight_ _Loving Kindness_

Code word or words:

Situations to recognize:

Loving Kindness

Day One

Day Two

Day Three

Day Four

Day Five

Day Six

Day Seven

The Exercise:

Forgiveness. This is the key that will unlock the chains that keep you from genuine loving kindness and hold you in bondage in bitter root judgment. Forgiveness will allow loving-kindness.

Being leaders in the ministry, we are able to witness many offenses by people that know they shouldn't hold an offense, or even get offended for that matter. Yet, how easy it is to become offended! I have to check myself, constantly, because being in the ministry is an area that allows many fiery darts to come my way. Before reconciliation can be attempted however, someone has gotten offended and they are leaving the church without a word. Now, the opportunity for unforgiveness lays barren as time goes by and dis-ease has an opportunity to sprout. It's a law. The promise is that any bitter root and unforgiveness will cause illness.

So, the first step is to forgive. Make a list of all the 'offenses' you have. Who offended you for and for what. Once you write them down, more often than not, they do not seem so important or drastic. Yes, you may have some serious offenses. But those, too need to be forgiven. We are to have unlimited forgiveness, not just when and where we desire. Yeshua tells us to forgive 70 x 7 (Matthew 18:22) which is a perfect and complete number.

Go through that list. Say out loud who you forgive and for what. The words you say carry great power. "I forgive my Dad/Mom/Uncle/Sister/Neighbor....for.....whatever they did or did not do. Now, let it go!

Our Messiah was accused and never defended Himself. He died on the stake so that we might be forgiven. Shouldn't we all be very humbled that He just didn't forgive us once? Or that He didn't just forgive the person next to us and not us but that He forgave everyone everything, at that moment. Those are two encompassing words: Everyone! Everything!

Honor is due Him. Great honor! And one way we can Honor the King is to honor His Word and forgive those who we are holding bitter root judgment against. It will and does release us of great bondage.

My husband, Jay had to learn to forgive his mother and father, too for that matter after his Dad committed suicide. He also had to forgive himself and see the loving-kindness that he needed to help the family mend. Was it easy? No. Was it a quick fix? No. But, he did it and it help everyone heal.

So, please, make that list. Say their names, forgive them. Now forgive yourself. God did not create you to lose. [1]

"She opens her mouth with wisdom and on her tongue is the law of kindness." Proverbs *Mishle 31:26*

"...to godliness brotherly kindness and to brotherly kindness, love." 2Peter *Kefa 1:7*

"There fore as the elect of God holy and beloved, put on tender mercies, kindness, humility, meekness, longsuffering, bearing with one another and forgiving one another if anyone has a complaint against another, even as Messiah forgave you so you also must do." Colossians 3:12,13.

"Do not let evil (hasatan, bitter root judgment, unforgiveness) *defeat you but defeat evil by doing good* (forgiveness, loving kindness).*"* Romans 12:21

Again, the thirteen loving-kindness attributes of God come from the book of Exodus as Moses asked God to see His glory. God agrees and passes before him calling out His character of loving-kindness. Realizing the divinity of self, realizing the divinity of others, nurturing creativity, provoke compassion, grace, to act with calmness, kindness, truth, protecting kindness, forgiveness of iniquity, forgiveness of transgression, forgiving mistakes, clearing of delusion. Exodus 33:19

Loving-kindness is an act, one that we physically need to do. Marcia Ford in the forward of Rabbi Rami Shapiro's book writes that loving-kindness is lived out in the relationship with others. That is so true.

In our congregation we are a concoction of many people and ethnic groups. It is through the mixture of these people, dress, hair, makeup, attitudes, sports – no sports, home school – public school, dance, or not, black, brown or white, and so on that we learn to cultivate loving kindness. A friend of mine who recently joined our congregation with her large family told me the other day that we are stretching them. And they are stretching us! And that's good! How else can we grow and truly learn to love others. And I mean truly love, not just say it but really love one another.

Look in your heart for bitterness. Hasatan knows that if he can get you offended and deceive you into harboring anger and bitterness that he can actually cause you to become locked in that place. You will lack loving kindness. Rabbi Sha'ul tells us in the book of Romans that the completion of Torah is love. *"Owe no one any matter except to love one another, for he who loves another has filled the Torah."* Romans 13:8 *"Love does no evil to a neighbor. Therefore, love is completion of the Torah."* Romans 13:10

You can do this. You are a perfect child of The Most High. You are a Holy Soul created to worship The King of the Universe in Holiness and perfection. You are His joy and He is our joy.

Choose Life!

1. Rabbi Ralph Messer, Simchat Torah Beit Midrash, Denver, CO

He who executes charity and injustice is regarded as though he had filled the entire world with kindness.

~ The Talmud

FINISHING THE CHARACTER TRAITS AND CHOOSING LIFE

PART THREE

"Now you shall say to the people, 'Says The Lord God YHWH, behold, I set before you the way of life and the way of death."
Jeremiah 21:8

Life/Death Good/Evil Blessings/Curses

Choose life!

The Phases of Mussar

Rabbi Yisrael Salanter documented and acknowledged that there are three main stages in the practice of Mussar. These three stages seem to be the strength of the whole character of Mussar.

Stages

Stage 1: Sensitivity, which the synonyms are: compassion, warmth, feeling, sympathy, understanding, and kindliness.

So, you must begin your journey with the understanding, sympathy, feeling, and sensitivity of each character/soul trait that you work on.

You will acquire sensitivity by addressing where the jealousy or fear comes into play. Why am I jealous? Why am I afraid? Alan Morinis talks about the sinking feeling in your heart when you see another being praised instead of yourself. It is that sinking feeling that births jealousy and envy. Being sensitive to that emotion will bring awareness and sensitivity to the inner part that is rising up to become jealous.

Stage 2: Self-discipline, which is: restraint, control, limit, and moderation. This is the point where our thoughts now become our action. We are aware and sensitive to the fact that we are jealous of a coworker who is receiving a promotion. Take that truth and process it into action. What am I really jealous of? I am jealous because I didn't get the promotion. The entire jealousy is based around 'self', around our own ego, around 'me'.

Now, process that into self-restraint, realizing that the sinking you feel is about yourself. Would you really want to take the promotion away from the coworker and give it to yourself? No, you wouldn't because our inner being is in fact pleased that our coworker, perhaps our friend has received a promotion and better pay. We are genuinely glad for that person. We have become sensitive to their needs, also. And we have now practiced self restraint in allowing ourselves to feel gladness for that person.

Stage 3: Transformation, which the synonyms are: to make over, alteration, change, conversion, and renovation. The Father and Yeshua make many references in Scripture to the heart and circumcision, as in one and the same.

The act of circumcision, or *Brit Milah*, is a status change. It is the sign of the Abrahamic Covenant. At that point of the circumcision his name was changed from Abram to Abraham. He opened his heart and was received into covenant with YHWH.

"And it came to be when Abram was ninety nine years old, that YHWH appeared to Abram and said to him, "I am El Shaddai – walk before Me and be perfect. And I give My covenant between Me and you and shall greatly increase you. And Abram fell on his face, and Elohim spoke with him, saying, 'As for Me, look, My covenant is with you and you shall become a father of many nations, And no longer is your name called Abram, but your name shall be Abraham, because I shall make you a father of many nations.'" Genesis *Bereshith 17:1-5*

"And Elohim said to Abraham, 'As for you, guard My covenant, you and your seed after you throughout their generations. This is My covenant which you guard between Me and you, and your seed after you: Every male child among you is to be circumcised. And you shall circumcise the flesh of your foreskin, and it shall become a sign of the covenant between Me and you.'" Genesis *Bereshith 17:9-11*.

In verse one, God tells Abraham to walk before Him and be perfect. He doesn't say to give it a good old college try. No, The Father desires that we are perfect, which we gain access to through The Son and The Torah – which are in fact the very 613 principles of God.

Yeshua gives us the very same command in Matthew *Mattithyahu* 5:48. *"Therefore, be perfect as your Father in the heavens is perfect."*

Jesus doesn't say to think about it.

And again we are cautioned about being perfect in 1John *Yohanan* 2:5. *"But whoever guards His Word, truly the love of Elohim has been perfected in him. By this we know that we are in Him."*

"Blessed are the perfect in the way, who walk in the teaching of YHWH." Psalms *Tehillim* 119:1.

Notice that we are perfect in Him, through Him, in His Word, in His Way, in His teachings, in His commands and in His love. Being perfect is not something we can accomplish on our own. Through the Great Comforter, The Holy Spirit, The *Ruach HaChodesh*, we are perfected and the layers of the onion are peeled away to reveal the inner core.

Sometimes it is an ugly sight, oh, that inner core of ours. But He is the Great Healer and He is The Great Revealer, too. He is *Yah Rapah* healer and *Yahovah Tsidkenu* Lord our righteousness.

To remove the skin in Hebrew is *ahriot*, which can be translated into harlotry. By removing the foreskin of our hearts, we are leaving behind, or removing (foreskin) the harlotry of our lives. The harlotry in our lives will represent the idols in our hearts, which is the reason that we are again admonished to circumcise the heart. Just think of that onion. The outer layer is crackly and awful to taste. The next layer is hard and bitter. As one delves deeper into the onion, the taste becomes sweeter and the texture is softer and just plain delicious.

To recap, the three stages are:
- Sensitivity and Compassion.
- Self-discipline and self-restraint.
- Transformation and renovation.

Recording

Be disciplined in writing in your journal every night. The points, *bechirah*, where you make the choice between the evil inclination, *yetzer ha'ra* and the good inclination *yetzer ha'tov* will help you to realize where your struggle takes place.

By becoming aware of the inclinations that make up the hundreds of choices that you make every day, you will see the pattern of the *bechirah*, the points that can control our thoughts and emotions.

Does anger flare up when a car cuts in front of you? Writing down the place in your emotion that caused the flare up helps us to recognize each tiny situation.

It is important to not make a person the focal point of your anger, such as: he makes me so angry when....or...oooo I get so mad when she....

What one is really saying in that situation is that the other person is not behaving in a manner in which is pleasing to *them*, or suitable to *them*. In that case, we are allowing our reactions to develop because of a certain person's character traits. We can not change any other person! We can only change ourselves and how we handle situations caused by other people.

Always, always turn the negative action into a positive action. Always try and work on a positive trait – that in of itself will slowly dismiss the negative trait. As the driver cuts in front of you – force yourself, if you must, to say a prayer, a blessing over that person. Maybe his wife is having a baby; maybe her child is sick at school. Maybe their bank account is short funds. Something might be out of place -something could be wrong, so replace that negative trait of anger, with a positive trait of compassion. Pray.

Practice

Work on each trait weekly, monthly and yearly. Accentuate on the positive, diminish the negative. As time goes by, you will realize that the character trait of fear is replaced with that of joy, and the trait of anger replaced with loving kindness. Acknowledge – resist – reverse.

Remember that life is a journey and there is always a big picture. Our souls are not motionless, they are ever changing and growing and cultivating. What we allow our souls to cultivate will greatly shape our habits, our futures and that of our children and the very people around us. Change is always taking place, and we are given free will in that change, we are given the opportunity of choice. Or we can remain in that season that we are in, always spinning and wondering…

I can choose to be jealous, or I can choose to wish her well.

In the teaching of Numbers *Bemidbar* 16, Pastor Howard of Simchat haMashiach Beit Emunah, brought up a very fine *bechirah*; a point. Qorah rose up before Moshe and assembled 'against' him; V.16:3, bringing other leaders of the congregation, men of authority and recognition to also rise up.

Qorah's jealousy enabled him to speak and organize other 'leaders' of the community to rise up against Moshe. His jealousy turned to anger, and eventually became death to him and those that followed that spirit of jealousy. Jealousy – anger – death. Is it today a spiritual death?

The very point that drove Qorah to jealousy is found in verse 16:3. He was denying the very existence of the Creator by stating that Moshe lifted *himself* up above the assembly of YHWH. The very fact that Qorah did not acknowledge God in this sequence of events, placed little or no importance on The Creator Himself. He took the very deity away from God that positioned Moses where he was in the first place. The idol of Qorah's heart became himself.

B'nei aliyah means 'those who ascend.' Yeshua being our example shows us that He descended before He ascended and that there is a descent before the ascent.

You are a Holy Soul, a part of the Creator, created in the likeness of the Great I AM. You can start your ascent.

Please, don't condemn yourself. This is not about how awful we are, or how wrong we've been. We have all messed up, and we have all been horrible. The enemy wants us to stay there, in that season. Just shout NO! We are going forward. It's about change. It's about going forward – forward with God. It's about the ascent.

Change Your Life

Keep your focus on changing yourself – not your spouse, children, mother, father, brother, sister, or friend. This is about changing and redirecting our own very personal character traits.

A little story:

We have five children. Our oldest is a firefighter, one level under a Paramedic; probably by the time this is printed he will be a Paramedic. He's a great guy, very calm and smart. I feel so at peace, to know that God has his life in His hands and a great woman in the plans for my son.

Our two youngest ones are guys, and very busy. School, sports, fun, video games, skate boarding, just plain busy little boys.

In between we have two daughters. At the writing of this, they are 18 and 20 and beautiful.

My husband says we have lots of flies buzzing around.

And we do.

July 4th weekend was havoc. Young men were everywhere – everywhere to be with our daughters. Needless to say 'The Dad Personality' came out in my husband.

I could not understand this 'The Dad Personality'. So, to make a long story short, we had a disagreement, simply due to the fact that I could not relate to this 'Dad Personality'. I had no idea where he was coming from and why he was so upset. A led to B, led to C and soon we were at Z. And then we asked ourselves; 'how did we get here?'

The moral of this little story? My reaction was off. I really did not understand where my husband was coming from in regards to his daughters, and I was not reacting to his emotions well at all. So, there is a key ingredient to change within us. Stop, listen, think and pray about what you are hearing, what you are feeling.

Now, four days and four sleepless nights later, I understand where my husband was coming from. But – I had to put my emotions, my knowledge and my reactions aside and listen through The Holy Spirit.

You can do this. We all want to better ourselves and I know that much if I know anything at all.

If you need support or just prayer, please email me: shmbe@joimail.com I'm here for you.

Eight More

There are eight more positive character traits that we can work on. These positive traits will absolutely reverse the negative traits in our lives.
- Gratitude
- Compassion
- Generosity
- Enthusiasm
- Honor
- Trust
- Faith
- Forgiveness

We too often love things and use people, when we should be using things and loving people. Unknown

Gratitude

Gratitude is a gift to those you love

Thankfulness is a force, it is an attitude. All around us there are those that are healthier, prettier, smarter, wealthier, taller, thinner, and happier. All around us are people that are less healthy, poor, fat, and depressed. We are a system of coexisting people, going here and there, looking and observing what we have or don't have. The 'haves' vs. the 'have-nots'.

Dr. Suess wrote a great book called *The Star Belly Sneeches*. There were sneeches with stars that wouldn't let the sneeches without the stars stand by the campfire to roast marshmallows. Along came a magic character and put stars on the bellies of the non starred sneeches. This caused great animosity amongst the starred sneeches and they had their stars removed. Then the other sneeches had their stars removed and around and around the story went. The stars on the bellies became the focus until no sneech knew who the original starred belly sneech was and who wasn't.

Gratitude is thankfulness to The Father for what we have. It is an action and a verb. It is also a choice. It is content-ness. We have a choice to focus on the deficiencies in our lives or we can focus on what we do have. There is really no limit of what we don't have. But, as Rabbi Bachya ibn Pakuda in *Duties of the Heart* teaches, there isn't a person alive who hasn't been given gifts. If only the gift of life and hope, it is still a huge gift from The Father.

"Baruch ata adonai, eloheinu melech ha'olam shehechiyanu v'kiyamanu v'higiyanu l'zman hazeh."

"Blessed are you O Lord our God, King of the Universe who has kept us in life, and sustained us and allowed us to reach this moment."

Alan Morinis teaches that the soul trait of gratitude holds the key to opening the heart. It is a soul trait that is superior and opens doors to the hearts of others. When we are thankful to God, we are honoring The King. When we show gratitude to others in our lives for their gifts to us, whatever they may be, even a smile, we are again honoring The King. An inner heart that is thankful will provide us with assets that help us face whatever we may come across in our lives.

Rabbi Messer teaches ten key points about thankfulness.[1]

1. It is a learned attitude
2. It is magnetic
3. It creates joyous people
4. It is created by focus
5. It is required to enter into the presence of God
6. It should occur because of the goodness of God, not because of perfect circumstances
7. It occurs when we remember good things God has done
8. It occurs when you replay memories of God's blessings
9. It occurs when we write notes of thankfulness
10. It occurs when we express out loud our gratitude

The goal in our lives is to weave thankfulness deep into our souls, for even the smallest of things.

A jealous heart will keep us from the gratitude in our lives that our spirit truly wants to feel. The Scriptures tell us that jealously, a desire and a pursuit of honor will keep us from the heavenly realm that we are to live in. A jealous person is the only one that suffers, not the person that he is jealous of. Jealousy will keep him from enjoying what God has given him and gratitude will be lost in a tangled emotional drag.

To be jealous of another's spiritual walk will also keep the jealous person from the walk that The Father has planned for him at that moment. Remember that Saul's anger towards David stemmed from his jealousy. Saul was riddled with jealousy and envy and it took control of his life.

Haman envied the favor that Mordecia was shown and Cain was jealous of Abel. Rachel was resentful of Leah and Josephs' brothers were extremely riddled with jealousy that turned to hate. There were dire consequences to all of these examples.

Thankfulness will die, for jealousy is an overpowering evil inclination, one that will eventually kill us. Remember, love does not envy; 1Corinthians 13:4.

One day after my 9 year olds' fiddle lesson, he wanted something to eat. We live in a very rural area, so the fast food places are extremely limited. I had little cash, which meant that the order I placed for him was in itself going to be restricted. He got a small chicken finger special through the drive in which consisted of one tiny chicken something of a strip. The box of ranch dressing was bigger than the strip. He said to me: "thank you mommy, it's better than nothing."

Wow! I know he was disappointed. I know he was probably expecting a big order of restaurant chicken strips. But, his reaction was that of a little boy 'thanks'.

Gratitude in Hebrew is *hakarat ha'tov* which means recognizing the good.

That is such a key statement: to recognize the good. There is good in everything, we just have to find it. We can't and shouldn't live in a Pollyanna world, but there *is* good in everything, for everything comes from The Father.

As you work on this trait, write in your journal everyday what you are grateful for – for just that day. Did you wake up? Did it rain and clear the air? Did you have a good lunch? Did a friend get well? Was a baby born? Did you find your other shoe? Did your check book balance? Did you have a hot shower? Did your mother call you? Did you get to work on time? Did you hear a bird sing?

Physically express your gratitude. Write a note to your banker, tip the waitress extra, call a friend. Hug your spouse, thank your children. Even pat your dog. Write that physical expression down in your journal and you will begin to see a pattern. You will also see, as you recap events, where you didn't thank some one, or at times that you were ungrateful.

Do not focus on the things or events that weren't or didn't happen. Focus on what did happen, what brought you joy, for there will be a lot in our lives that won't happen, if we look at our lives through our human eyes and mindset.

"And you shall eat and be satisfied and shall bless YHWH your Elohim for the good land which He has given you." Deuteronomy *Debarim* 8:10.

"Raise a shout for YHWH
All the earth
Serve YHWH with gladness
Come before His presence with singing
Know that YHWH He is Elohim
He has made us and we are His People and the sheep of His pasture
Enter into His gates with thanksgiving
And into His courts with praise
Give thanks to Him; bless His Name
For The Lord He is good
And His kindness is everlasting
And His truth endures to all generations."

Psalms *Tehillim* 100.

Gam zu l' tovah And that is also for good

1. Rabbi Ralph Messer Simchat Torah Beit Emunah

Change Your Life

<u>Notes</u>　　　　　<u>*Week Nine*</u>　　　　<u>*Gratitude*</u>

Code word or words:

Situations to recognize:

Gratitude

Day One

Day Two

Day Three

Day Four

Day Five

Day Six

Day Seven

The Exercise:
Each day write down one thing that you were grateful for. It doesn't have to be grand, even a small thing. Did you make the green light? Did your check book balance? Did you hug your children? Did your feet hit the floor this morning? Did your spouse wake up?

If you have had a bad day, someone in this world has had a worse day and that is a guarantee. Write down what aggravated you, and out of that aggravation write down what small accomplishment for The Father you may have actually done.

Each day, try and call some one, or speak to some one and tell them that you are thankful that they are in your life. Even if you two aren't particularly fond of one another, for iron sharpens iron, and if it wasn't for people, we'd all be lonely wanderers, assuming that we had all the answers.

At the writing of this book, my husband and I are going through the latter teenage years. Opposites of the sex are coming in to play, emotions are high, dynamics are many and questions that aren't easy to answer are being asked.

I wish I could lock my children away until that perfect spouse arrives hand delivered by God, knocking at my door. "God sent me to marry_____and here I am. I have a job, a good salary, I am in Torah, I love children, I love in-laws. I'll never argue with her, and never make her cry. I'll take care of your daughter forever, and we'll have all the feast days with you."

But I know that is not realistic. So, for this day, I am grateful, I am telling myself to be grateful for the dynamics that we are going through. I know God is in control, and this will make me a better person. And my husband, too!

If a day goes by and you can not find anything to be grateful for, there is a spiritual block. Ask God to remove that and He will. He desires our love and our thankfulness. Go over the 10 points listed in this chapter. You'll become aware of all that you truly have without even having.

Thankfulness is an expression of God

Compassion

"And having seen the crowds, He was moved with compassion for them, because they were weary and scattered as sheep having no shepherd." Matthew *Mattithyahu* 9:36

Compassion, sympathy, empathy, grace and mercy. *Chesed.* Notice in Matthew 9:36 we are told that Yeshua was *moved* with compassion. Compassion becomes an action, an act or a reaction that we can take part in. It is more than just a feeling of being sorry for someone.

"But You O YHWH, are a compassionate El and showing favor, patience and great in kindness and truth." Psalms *Tehillim* 86:15.

"The Lord shows favor and is compassionate patient and great in kindness." Psalms *Tehillim* 145:8

"And when the Master saw her He had compassion on her and said to her, 'Do not weep.'" Luke 7:13

In the Scriptures we are told that the Lord has compassion, is full of compassion, had compassion, having compassion and moved with compassion. Deuteronomy 13:17, Psalms 78:38, Micah 7:19, Matthew 14:14, Matthew 20:34 Mark 8:2, 1Peter 3:8.

As we can see, compassion did not begin in the New Testament as sometimes we are taught. God is a compassionate El, a merciful God, full of grace and mercy, *chesed.* He is *Yahovah Jireh* our provider.

"...but showing mercy to thousands to those who love Me and guard my commands." Exodus *Shemoth* 20:6

God's mercy can be seen, it is shown, it will endure forever, it will not be withheld, and it will save us. We will rejoice against judgment and it is something we may obtain in righteousness to reap in mercy. Mercy will return as mercy and kindness are one, and His mercy is great. His mercy shall not depart and He will have mercy upon the afflicted. God desires mercy not sacrifice, there is a mercy seat of pure gold, He remembers His mercy, His mercy and truth go before us, we trust in the mercy, we hope in the mercy, and His throne is up held by mercy. Grace, mercy and peace are from God, and according to His mercy He saved us. He is gracious, merciful and slow to anger.

In the Strong's Exhaustive Concordance there are 2 ¾ columns of the word mercy and merciful.

Mercy, compassion, and grace go hand in hand with truth and trust. We receive the trust in The Father, the truth of His word, and the grace and compassion that He bestows upon us because we are walking in His Truth.

Rachamim is the Hebrew word for compassion and shares it's root with the word *rechem,* which means 'womb'. Isn't that amazing that we are connected with compassion as a mother is connected to her unborn child within her?

A very well know term to describe God is *Ha'Rachaman* – The Compassionate One and *Ha'El Ha'Av Ha'Rachaman-* God the Compassionate Father. Just as an earthly father has compassion on his children, so does God The Father have compassion on us.

Since we are created in the likeness and the image of God, He can feel our pain, just as when Yeshua wept over Lazarus and wept over Jerusalem.

In that same likeness, we are to feel our fellow man's pain. That is why compassion is an action. Alan Morinis stated it so well in his book, that for *chesed* to be real we must take action to uphold that other person. Likewise, *rachamim,* compassion, does not come into being just by feeling empathy.

We are to express our compassion for one another by the actions we take. It is not enough to just feel sorry for some one. Action is required otherwise we become observers of life.

A very good friend of mine lost her 18 year old son from a motor cross accident, going over a jump he had gone over a thousand times. He went too high, too fast and came down crushing his chest, smashing his face, and biting off his tongue. The parents were right inside the house, and came out to see their only son lying on the ground. He was flown to the hospital, but was not to live.

This young man was a warrior; he did everything with gusto, even dying. I can try to understand how horrible it would be to lose a son, I have three. But I can not feel, truly feel the depth of her pain. I guess it will never go away, it may subside, but it will always be a shadow in her life. My compassion towards her is that I sometimes say nothing, sometimes we hug. Or cry. If she is sad, I am not joyful. If she is happy, I laugh with her. If she is angry, she can be angry at me, go ahead! Punch me, it's okay!

My compassion has to become an action, so she can physically feel it and see it.

The Book of Numbers, Moses explains the cities of refuge that God commanded there be. God had/has such compassion that He had cities of refuge given in order to protect someone that had accidentally killed another fellow human. Yes, there are consequences, but compassion abounds.

There is *Tzedakah* and *Chesed* within our Holy God, Blessed Be He. While *Tzedakah* is a gift of a physical thing as an item, money or food, *Chesed* is the gift of the person.

Think of the cherubs facing one another on the Ark. It was between the two cherubs that God spoke to Moses. The message of this representation was so important that it was deemed by God Himself to be adequate to prevail over the risk of misunderstanding. So, here we see that God speaks where two persons turn their face to one another in: love, embrace, generosity, care, and compassion. Face to face.

Rabbi Messer of Simchat Torah teaches to be careful how you treat the blood. We have Yeshua in us, I look at you I see Him, how I treat you is how I am treating Him. That puts a whole different perspective on the situation. If you are unkind, you are not unkind solely to me; you are unkind to God The Father, Yeshua The Son.

A sage taught something very interesting about the Holy Land. There are two seas in Israel; the Dead Sea and the Sea of Galilee. The latter is full of life: fish, birds, vegetation. The former as its name suggests, contains no life at all. Yet they are both fed by the same river, the Jordan. The difference is, he said, is that the Sea of Galilee receives water at one end and gives out water at the other. The Dead Sea receives but does not give. The Jordan ends there. To receive without reciprocating is a kind of death. To live is to give.

Gratitude, compassion and the next chapter, generosity work together.

In your journal writing on compassion, make a list of the many verses in the Scriptures of compassion and mercy.

Remember compassion is an act, a deed. Simply praying for someone is an act of compassion. If you are lacking in compassion, write down in your journal why. What is spiritually blocking you? Why can't you relate? Do you not care for that person? Are you too busy with your own problems? Stop what you are doing and pray for that person. Send them a card, a Scripture verse. Or, just pray. Compassion comes in many forms. Feel it, breathe it.

Change Your Life

| *Notes* | *Week Ten* | *Compassion* |

Code word or words:

Situations to recognize:

Compassion

Day One:

Day Two:

Day Three:

Day Four:

Day Five:

Day Six:

Day Seven:

Exercise:

While you are writing in your journal each night, list for the next day what you can do to fulfill the act of compassion. Is there some one who needs prayer? Is there a need in your church or neighborhood?

Mrs. Messer of Simchat Torah Beit Midrash, without even knowing it, taught me a great lesson in compassion. She in passing conversation told me that whenever she drives past another car pulled off to the side of the road by a policeman, she says a prayer for that person.

What compassion! Have you ever had a ticket? I have – and it is an awful feeling, sitting in your car while a policeman asks for your i.d., registration and insurance (which for some reason I can never find at that moment).

If compassion is blocked for you, make a note of that. What in your heart is blocking it? What stops your feelings for another? Is the root jealousy or anger or bitterness? Seek it out, and again, The Holy Spirit will lead you through it.

Touch someone with a prayer –
they'll feel it

Generosity

> What is a Jewish sweater? It is the garment worn by a child when his mother is cold.

My mother is a remarkable woman. At the writing of this chapter she is 89 she is still quite spunky. She is that woman that made me wear a sweater when *she* was cold. She is forever trying to get us to eat the food off of her plate, and insisting that we haven't eaten enough.

There is a verse in the Scriptures that define Gods' love and His generosity and charity. *"As one whom his mother comforts, so I comfort you. And in Jerusalem, you are comforted."* Isaiah *Yeshayahu* 66:13.

Have you ever been cold, or hungry or scared? A blanket is a great comfort. A hot cup of soup soothes the soul. A prayer chases away the fear.

Our Messiah taught us these and gave us these. He fed the hungry; he healed the deaf, blind, sick and leprous. He cried with Miriam and Martha. He prayed over His City and His People. He gave until he died and now He gives more.

Generosity has got to be giving from the heart. When we have idols in our heart, it will block us from giving. The Hebrew wording for that is *timtam ha'lev:* a blocked up heart. The opposite is *nedivut ha'lev* – the generosity of the heart.

Our past can also keep us from giving from our hearts. Our past shapes the kindness of the heart or the lack of. Unforgiveness, bitterness, bitter root judgment, anger, depression, lack of joy, sadness and anger are blocks to our generosity. The win/ lose mentality of this culture can also act as a huge block. All of these emotions keep us from giving to one another and they keep our heart sealed, blocked and closed. In essence, we are uncircumcised.

It is impossible to receive if one can not give. To give is to receive and to receive is to give.

Yeshua was always giving. He was never needy. He was never expecting. He never lacked of His perfect giving. He gave Himself right to the end, and He continues to give.

The Hebrew term *Tzedakah* is a righteous form of giving in the Hebrew culture. In our synagogue/church, we have a *Tzedakah* Box in the back, where members of our congregation generously give 'from the heart'. We do not ask, but rely on the giving of the heart spurred on by the Holy Spirit to give. Through that then we give to those in need. Even those that need the finances, are able to give of themselves in the congregation, whether it be in prayer, helping to clean, working with the youth, singing, whatever. There is always something to give. Even a word of encouragement.

Generosity doesn't have to be cash. Do you have extra time? Give time. Do you have extra food? Give food. Do you have extra blankets? Give blankets. Do you have an abundance of firewood? Give wood.

Generosity reaches past our desires and into the many realms of caring. The Talmud teaches that the greatest charity is to enable the poor to earn a living, to say little and do much. And even a poor man who lives off charity can perform acts of charity.

The Ba'al Shem Tov teaches that to generously bear the burden of others is the key theme of generosity.

Rabbi Sha'ul writes that we are to bear the burdens of others, in Galatians 6:2, 3. Of course, The Messiah to this day, bears all of our burdens.

The fingers of generosity claim territory that we can't even imagine living in this culture.

God emphasizes His generosity in many ways. He tells His people to leave the corners of the field. We are to leave the field on a Sabbatical; we are to let those glean. In the 7th year debt is forgiven, and in the year of Jubilee land is returned to the owner. God has cities of refuge, places of rest, and He freely gives inheritance. What extreme generosity!

"But the mercy of The Lord is from everlasting to everlasting upon them that fear Him and His righteousness to children's children." Psalms *Tehillim* 103:17

If you are not a generous person, start small. Go out and have an inexpensive lunch. A bowl of soup, a salad, something that won't cost you a lot, but tip generously and abundantly.

Whatever church or synagogue you go to, try something daring. Put cash into the offering, tithe, or Tzedakah box and do not expect a receipt. Just give. Let the Lord distribute it.

If you were going to purchase steaks and decided not to, purchase them anyway and give them to someone.

In James 2:15, 16 we are admonished to do something, to not just talk. And in Galatians 6:10 we are to take every opportunity to do good works, *mitzvohs'*. Any unselfish action will cause thankfulness and give glory to God, 2Corinthians 9:11.

Reach into your soul, heart, pockets and life and give of it. Pray and seek His Wisdom, He will guide you in your generosity.

Notes Week Eleven Generosity

Code word or words:

Situations to recognize:

Generosity

Day One:

Day Two:

Day Three:

Day Four:

Day Five:

Day Six:

Day Seven:

The Exercise:

This takes pre planning. If you by trade are not a generous person, you can create a new habit within you to become generous. Generosity does not have to come by way of just the wallet either. Being generous with your time, with your compassion, with your wisdom, knowledge, property and other daily items can go a long way.

You can give someone a ride; you can accompany an elderly person to the doctor's office. There are many possibilities! Seek out your potential; let the idea become the act. Let it become a verb.

The night before, write in your journal for that following day an area where you can be generous. Think about all of the possibilities and all areas of giving.

And again, write in your journal about that day of the accounts where you were generous. There is also the exercise to write down the accounts that you were not generous. By doing this you will be able to see your habits when it comes to generosity, where you are lacking and where you are not. Some people can easily write a check but not give of their time. It is an interesting concept, time vs. money. Hoarding lacks in wisdom, yet spending over the budget is equally unwise. The challenge is that time is not our own and our possessions come from Him. The Lord desires that we are generous with both to His children.

"Then The King will say to those on His right, 'Come, you whom my Father has blessed, take your inheritance, the Kingdom prepared for you from the founding of the world. For I was hungry and you gave me food, I was thirsty and you gave me something to drink, I was a stranger and you made me your guest. I needed clothes and you provided them, I was sick and you took café of me, I was in prison and you visited me.' Then the people who have done what God wants will reply, 'Lord, when did we see you hungry and feed you, or thirsty and give you something to drink? When did we see you a stranger and make you our guest or needing clothes and provide them? When did we see you sick or in prison, and visit you? The King will say to them, 'Yes! I tell you that whenever you did these things for one of the least important of these brothers of mine, you did them for me!" Matthew *Matityahu* 25:34-40. (David Stern's Complete Jewish Bible) That's Torah!

Cast your bread upon the waters for after many days you will find it ~ Solomon

Enthusiasm

"For he put on righteousness as a breastplate and a helmet of salvation upon his head; and he put on the garments of vengeance for clothing and was clad with zeal as a cloak." Isaiah 59:17 KJV

Eagerness, zeal, interest, keenness, fervor, passion, gusto, zest, dedication, vehemence and *zerizut* in Hebrew. These are descriptive words that should describe the way we live.

In the Hebrew mindset, The Walk of God is an action, a way of life. It is not a belief system. Is my walk with zeal? Or am I sluggish, slumped over. When you see a person walking to exercise, to strengthen their heart, are they walking slowly? Or are they walking with speed, their head is straight and their arms are moving in rhythmic motion. It is a smooth site, one with dignity, purpose and enthusiasm. Zeal!

We are taught that the trait of zeal is the base of all the other traits. To have joy, one must have passion. To have kindness and charity and be giving, one must have enthusiasm.

King David was quick to obey the commandments. Daniel was quick to pray. Rabbi Sha'ul was quick to obey Yeshua. Noah didn't question and ponder the instructions to build the ark. Abraham didn't hesitate when he was told to take Isaac to the mountain.

Enthusiasm is a key to life and zeal is described as intense enthusiasm.

My daughter Hannah told me that you 'get' enthusiasm when you get inspired. I thought about that statement and her as I watch her play the fiddle and as I watch her sing in the praise team. There is great enthusiasm, and great inspiration.

What gives us inspiration? People. When Hannah is playing her fiddle, there is constant clapping, or clapping at the end. When she is singing in the praise team with her hands raised, there is enthusiasm from the congregation to worship YHWH along with her.

In different settings, she has played music for non enthusiastic people, and her enthusiasm drains for it is difficult to maintain the stage presence of complete liveliness when the crowd is uninterested.

The other day we took a young soon to be married couple to lunch. The young man sat at the table, hunched over, elbows on the table, hat on sideways, no job, no skills, and no interest. By the end of the lunch I felt drained.

People are energized or de-energized by other people. Rabbi Messer teaches that we are like conductors, and we either illuminate each other or we drain one another.

Have you ever been around someone who is just so full of life? Your spirit craves that energy – you get a lift. Have you ever been around someone that is stirring up strife, gossiping, or bored with life? (Remember the old teachers' quote: Those that are bored are boring). Gossiping will wear us down, it will drain our conductor.

There seems to be a laziness or a heaviness with people that are not or are never enthusiastic. As in the young man at the restaurant in the above story. Even his physical demeanor was that of a heavy spirit. I just wanted to shout: Get happy! Enjoy your ice tea! What a great lunch! You could be dead!

My other daughter Sophie told me that enthusiasm is thinking about the future and what she can contribute to it. She also suggested that enthusiasm is answering a question with more than one word.

"How are you?"

"Fine."

Or:

"How are you?"

"I'm great! Praise God!"

The reason why I included my two daughters in this chapter is because they were there at this particular lunch. On one side of me are two cheery, enthusiastic, embracing-life, working for God young adults. On the other side was a very unenthusiastic man, even for The Lord.

When there is a lack of enthusiasm it can create a laziness. Laziness will consume our own life strength, Ecclesiastics 4:5 and laziness produces waste, Proverbs 18:9.

The most important thing that we can be enthusiastic about is The Messiah, Yeshua. If nothing else, start your day with zeal towards Him. Thank you YHWH that I am alive. Woo Hoo!

"Whatsoever thy hand findeth to do, do it with thy might for there is no work, nor device, nor knowledge, nor wisdom in the grave where thou goest." Ecclesiastics. 9:10 KJV

Notes   *Week Twelve*   *Enthusiasm*

Code word or words:

Situations to recognize:

Change Your Life

<u>*Enthusiasm:*</u>

Day One

Day Two

Day Three

Day Four

Day Five

Day Six

Day Seven

The Exercise:

My children were hired to play Irish music for a wedding. My son, the firefighter had to make a trade of shift to play, and the three of them had to learn some difficult chords. It would encompass dress rehearsal Friday night, setting up sound, and 3 hours of playing. His enthusiasm was dragging. In the morning before the bride came to hear their set list and settle on an amount, we talked about zeal and enthusiasm.

He expressed to me his lack of enthusiasm for this particular venue and that he wasn't going to pretend to be happy.

To pretend to be happy. That sentence really spoke to me.

How often do we confuse 'happiness' with being content. However, the Thesaurus lists 'content' as one of the synonyms of 'happy'. To have joy, we have joy in The Father. To have peace, we have peace in Him. To be content, we are content through Him.

Each week, my ten year old has to a list of spelling words and vocabulary words. He has to check and double check the meanings of the vocabulary words and then writes a couple brief sentences in his own words about what they mean to him. One list included 'contentment'. His sentences amazed me – oh the mind of a child! "I am content that I don't have a phone." And "I am content to be the youngest in the family."

Good thoughts – and what contentment.

It all depends on our relationship, not religion, with The Father and His Son. We even derive our 'happiness' on Him, for He is in control of all things.

The Hebrew word for happy *esher* comes from the root *ashar*: to be level, to be right, to go forward, to be honest, bless.

Zeal in Hebrew is *qin'ah*, coming from the root *qana*: jealous, envious, to be moved, to be zealous, jealousy (x) sake. In the NT the word is *zelos*, from *zeo*: in favor, sense, ardor, and jealousy as of a husband or God, envy, a fervent mind.

If you put these words and meanings together, we can draw a very picturesque definition of our walk, our life how it should be and The God that we serve.

We are enthusiastic for God; we have zeal for Him and His walk, His word, His ways. He are jealous for Him. Not of Him or because of Him, but for Him. We are happy, moving forward, blessed, content for Him, because of Him, with Him, through Him.

Our happiness creates enthusiasm – our enthusiasm creates our happiness.

As you work on this trait, start small if you tend to not be an overly enthusiastic person. Write down in your journal or this book, one day at a time what you will be enthusiastic about. That evening meditate on that particular incident and search the why's and how's of that 'enthusiastic' moment.

We all know that it is hard to have zeal about paying bills, ok, so that's a given. But, if you look towards the end result – you're done with paying bills! – then what contentment you will have.

The most important thing that we as Torah and Yeshua believers can give to this world is zeal: for The Father and His Word. Tell those around you what you are for – not what you are against. (Rabbi Messer). We need to shine for Yeshua and have enthusiasm to bless His Holy Name.

At the work place, do your coworkers see energy? Or do they see someone complaining and lacking in their duties.

Keep a strict journal in regards to this trait. Again, you will see a pattern, and by realization and honesty you can deal with your zeal or lack of it.

"Yuk – I have to go to the dentist (forgive me if any of your are a dentist or married to one….) Ok, so the realizations is that we don't have much zeal about going to the dentist. Okay, then ….when we are DONE – we're DONE! Have zeal!

I lived through the dentist! Thank you Jesus!

Every man is enthusiastic at times. One man has enthusiasm for thirty minutes, another has it for thirty days – but it is the man that has it for thirty years who makes a success in life. Unknown

Honor

Who is honored? He who honors others.

Pirkei Avos Ethics of The Fathers [1]

To honor another is the contradiction that we encounter for we know that as believers we should not seek to be honored. Yet, by honoring others we are indeed honored. A friend's honor should be as dear to us as our own for it is truly by honoring others that we earn honor for ourselves.

Rabbi Messer of Simchat Torah Beit Midrash in Denver, CO has a lunch set up for guests, Pastors, people in his congregation, and friends. It is called the Rabbi's table.

I'll never forget the first time I was included in the Rabbi's Table.

It was our first visit at Simchat Torah, November of 2004. After the service, the ushers came and retrieved all seven of us, my husband and our five children, and led us to an upstairs room. The table was glorious! - complete with white linen, gold rimmed dinner plates, refreshing glasses of ice tea and a most superb luncheon. There were approximately twenty of us, a mixture of guests. He and Mrs. Messer were gracious hosts and my family and I were honored to dine with him and his other guests. He treated the women like true ladies, and he was encouraging and polite and talkative to the gentlemen. Enthusiasm!

I believe that he does this every Sabbath, including a combination of guests, some from out of town, and some from his own congregation.

In addition, during the Sabbath Services, Rabbi Messer is quick to introduce guests, quick to ask them to pray or speak. He is quick to honor.

It is because of that, and including other character traits of him, that I see people going out of their way to honor him. In his humility, he allows it, but never placing himself above those that honor him. He truly is a mentor in honoring others as he gives us the example of not seeking honor for himself but seeking to honor others that come into his life.

Each and every one of us is created by The Creator. Each and every one of us is a Holy Soul, neither produced by another, nor created by man. Therefore, honor and dignity is due each and every one of us and not because of the vastness of our achievements, but because each of us is a Holy Soul, God's creation in His perfectness.

Honor in Hebrew is *Kavod, Kabowd, kabod;* good sense, splendor, copiousness, glorious, glory, honor. *Tipharah, tiph'ereth;* ornament, beauty, bravery, comely, fair, glory, honor. *Yaqar, yeqar;* to make rare, precious, be prized, to set by, value, precious things, price, glory, and honor.

In the New Testament it is *timao, time';* to honor, value, revere, dignity, precious, price and valuable. Consider the meanings of these words. There is only one entity that I know of that fulfills all of these synonyms – YHWH. It certainly isn't me.

In Proverbs we are told that before honor is humility. A Psalm says that His horn (Yeshua) will be honored; and throughout Scripture we are commanded to honor our parents.

In the Book of John, chapters 5 and 8 Yeshua explains what *Kavod* is, how we are to react and act to it because of it and through it. Yeshua gives us the example that our honor goes to the Father in all things. When we honor another, we do in fact honor The Father. We honor the King.

Yet, according to Rabbi Salanter, there is a fine line between the honor we ought to give other souls, and the honor that our own ego desires. Rabbi Salanter sites the sages counsel to flee from honor.[2] He also states that honor is one of the factors that can drive a person out of this world. We can become so focused on the honor of our selves and of our self, that we literally can die a physical or spiritual death.

The paradox here is, while we are to flee from honor, we are to bring honor to others. And what if they flee and how do we flee?

The point in case could be the luncheon that Rabbi Messer holds for different guests and congregants at Simchat Torah. Suppose after his invitation, I would have declined the offer, stood steadfast where I was seated, and denied him the graciousness of offering my family and I a wonderful lunch.

Number one, I could have possibly hurt his feelings. Number two, he could have possibly taken my attitude as wrong, as accusatory. And lastly, more importantly, would I have been so self-important in my humility to deny any account of graciousness, kindness or honor that Rabbi Messer was wanting to offer me that I would instead actually honor myself from the ego of my self. "I'm too humble to be honored at your luncheon…" Indeed a fine line. So, we turn that around and offer gratitude and thankfulness for his hospitality.

The opposite of honoring another is to bring shame to them. Often times, by shaming another, we try or think we try, to elevate and honor ourselves.

"And He also spoke this parable to some who relied on themselves that they were righteous, and looking down on others: 'Two men went up to the Set apart Place to pray – the one a Pharisee and the other a tax collector. The Pharisee stood and began to pray with himself this way, 'Elohim, I thank You that I am not like the rest of men, swindlers, unrighteous, adulterers, or even as this tax collector. I fast twice a week; I give tithes of all that I possess.' But the tax collector standing at a distance would not even raise his eyes to the heaven, but was beating his breast saying, 'Elohim, show favor unto me, a sinner!' 'I say to you, this man went down to his house declared right, rather than the other. For everyone who is exalting himself shall be humbled, and he who is humbling himself shall be exalted.'" Luke 18:9-14

We who walk in the Kingdom and the Glory of God should not even think of taking our ego to that point where we ridicule or condemn others by stroking ourselves. God has an uncanny way of offering measure for measure and our self honor will come back to bite us – hard.

Mussar teaches that our character traits need to be actions rather than feelings. Feelings keep us bottled up in self; such as:

I feel so bad for that person….I'm so sad for him….I feel horrible that they…. The main thrust of the 'feeling' is 'I'. How I feel, how it is influencing 'me'. Poor little ol' me. But when we turn these character traits into an action, we remove the 'I' from the story and replace it with the: him/her or them.

A true test of honoring someone is how we react when another is honored above us, as in a job promotion, a contest, at church or just everyday life. Are we genuinely happy and joyful for that person? Or are we wondering ever so quietly why 'I' didn't get that promotion.

Honoring one another can be as simple as greeting someone. When we take the initiative to offer a smile, a good morning, a hello, we are in fact giving honor to them. Try a simple test: the next time you are on the phone with a faceless person – we've all been there - ask them how they are, how they are doing today. You will be pleasantly surprised at how genuinely astonished they are that you even asked!

Kavod also means glory. In the Torah portion, *Re'eh* – See; it speaks of giving Glory To The Father, in our obedience, the foods we eat, the High Holy Days we keep and honor, and the rest that He has given us.

There are seven presences where the Glory, The *Kavod,* The Honor of YHWH is.[3]

1. Adam/ The Garden
2. Noah/ The Ark
3. Moses/ The Tabernacle
4. The Temple
5. The Second Temple
6. Yeshua/Jesus as He walked
7. Yeshua/Jesus within us

In regards to number seven, we see that now the Glory of God is within us, and within the brother or sister next to us. The glory within us is our potential within us. And if it is within us, it is within our brothers and sisters, too. How wonderful it would be if we took the time to help another find their potential, to encourage another by honoring them, even by bringing someone a cup of coffee at synagogue.

Honor, humility and glory are wrapped up into a packaged deal. It is through remembering that, that we can truly separate our ego, our narrow mind from honoring ourselves.

There is only one that should receive Glory "I come to glorify the Father," Yeshua tells us.

To walk in humility before the Lord, and by honoring others we honor The King.

1. Pirkei Avos, The Ethics of The Fathers
2. Everyday Holiness The Path of Mussar, Alan Morinis
3. Rabbi Ralph Messer Simchat Torah Beit Midrash, Denver CO

Change Your Life

<u>Notes</u>   <u>Week Thirteen</u>   <u>Honor</u>

Code word or words:

Situations to recognize:

Vickie Howard

<u>*Honor:*</u>

Day One

Day Two

Day Three

Day Four

Day Five

Day Six

Day Seven

The Exercise:

This is very easy. In every situation as you work on this character trait, just ask yourself, 'am I honoring The Father by my behavior, by my thoughts and by my actions'?

If there is any doubt, the answer is probably not. My mother used to tell me that if I had to ask the price of a dress I probably couldn't afford it. And she would follow it up with: when in doubt – don't.

The fifth Commandment of God is to honor your father and your mother. It is a commandment with a promise of a long life on the land. If you have children, you can show them how to honor by you honoring your parents. Wherever they are in this world, whether walking with Yeshua, in Torah, or in prison, we can show honor to our parents by not judging them, gossiping about them, slandering them or speaking evil of them. At all – and especially around our children! They in turn will learn this Torah principle.

By listening to another (unless it is *lashon ha'rah*) is an added simple way to honor someone. Just listen to their story. Be quiet, be still. Do not try to top their story. That is an influence of the Jezebel spirit.

Being on time is also a way to honor someone who is waiting for you. When we are late for an appointment, we dishonor the doctor, dentist, lawyer, and mechanic or whoever. Even if they make us wait seemingly hours in the waiting room, I can not use that as an excuse or reason for my tardiness.

As you write in your journal, make specific notes about honoring someone who you will come in contact with that day. If you have an appointment – be on time. Or call if you will be late. Greet the person next to you, on the phone or behind the cash register.

For the evening writing, jot down what possibly in a daily situation caused you to want to be honored, and you will find a common thread. It could be one of many emotions; that of jealousy, or lack of attention, such as abandonment. Jealousy is usually at the top of the list.

Jealousy is a gate that opens the thread of us wanting to be honored. Lucifer went through the gate of jealousy for he presumptuously wanted the honor and glory that YHWH was and is and is to come. His jealousy will ultimately lead to his death. So will our jealousy and envy – eventually lead to our own spiritual death?

"And call upon Me in the day of distress – Let Me rescue you and you esteem Me." Psalms *Tehillim* 50:15.

What a wonderful Scripture verse. We call upon Him in our distress, He will rescue us, and then we will esteem, honor, *kavod*, give glory to Him. That is the quintessential golden thread of The Scriptures; The God we serve and us. To give is to honor Him.

We call. He rescues. We honor.

And after this I heard a loud voice of a great crowd in the heaven saying, "Halleluyah! Deliverance and esteem and glory and honor and power to YHWH our Elohim!"

Revelation 19:1

Trust

"See, El is my deliverance; I trust and am not afraid. For Yah, YHWH is my strength and my song; and He has become my deliverance." Isaiah *Yeshayahu* 12:2

Trust is a multi-level emotion that runs in different stages through our lives.

Trust begins with birth, as we develop our screaming ability instantly and our mother picks us up and nurtures us, we trust her.

When we are small, we have complete trust in our parents, or caregiver. We trust our teachers, the bus driver, the police and the firefighter.

As we enter teenage years, we place our trust in diverse areas, such as the cell phone, iPODS, our peers, the internet, the music we listen to, the car we drive or ride in, our boyfriend or girlfriend, and in an unusual way and often distant, our parents.

Growing with years, we lean on our coworkers, the friends in our lives, our spouses, our banker, our doctors, dentists, our neighbors, and police when we need them, but not when we are speeding, and always we trust the firefighter.

As we age, we put trust into our children, our spouses, our favorite news anchor, our Pastor or Rabbi, our favorite grocer, our financial advisor, our health care specialist and our religious beliefs.

During our dotage years we trust in our grown children, our grand children, our caregivers, our doctors and our spouses. As we die, most of us turn to trust in God.

All of these areas that we place our trust in are fragile points in our lives for they can be broken and shattered.

Parents can abuse or leave their children. Boyfriends and girlfriends can break up. Police can become crooked. Cars will break down and mechanics will cheat us. Bus drivers will crash, and Pastors and Rabbis can fall. Teachers can molest. Firefighters can become alcoholics, bankers may steal, news anchors can lie, neighbors might sue, spouses can divorce, and children can run away. Caregivers can abuse, religions will let us down and death will eventually come.

"But, I trusted them!" Encircles our brain as we try to find some sort of relief from the pain that grips us as we realize our trust was broken. And, we should be able to trust our banker, the police, the teachers, and the religious leaders. But, they too, are imperfect humans in an imperfect world, where influences can grasp them and lead them astray.

The word for trust in Hebrew is *bitachon* which comes from the root word, *batach*, and meaning: confidence, refuge, to hope, be bold, secure or sure. Another form of trust used in the Scriptures is *chacah*, to flee for protection, to confide in, to have hope or to make refuge. And a third Hebrew word is *mibtach*; a refuge, security, assurance, confidence, hope, sure and trust.

The first time the word trust in English is used in Scriptures is in Judges 9:15. There are two different translations: *take shelter in my shade* and *come and put your trust in my shadow*.

The next verse is Ruth 2:12: *"YHWH repay your work and your reward is complete from YHWH Elohim of Yisrael under whose wings you have come to seek refuge."* (trust)

This verse sets the premise of where we are to trust and to whom.

The only entity that we are told to trust in is The Lord.

In the Book of Psalms, we are again reminded that fear and trust go hand in hand. *"You who fear YHWH, trust in YHWH."* Psalms *Tehillim* 115:11. Fear = awe = *yirah*.

If we keep our focus on the LORD and not those around us, or our properties, or planes, or vehicles or even spouses, our trust is in truth. For He is The Truth, He is never wavering.

When we put our trust into people, we then have expectations, and we will undoubtedly be let down. And then, we may confuse those disappointments with our emotions targeted at God, and here comes that old line: 'Oh, I can't trust anyone, not even God.' How arrogant is that statement! That feeling creates a sense of loneliness, of oneness, of superiority, if you will. A false sense of "I'm the only one I can trust….no one can do it as good as me…"

It's not The Father that let us down, or caused us grief, or disappointment or pain, or hurt, or betrayal or any other emotion that we might feel after someone whom we placed trust in let us down. When we react to someone's unworthiness in a blame state, we set the scene for a 'self-mode'. "I was let down." And yes, that may be true, however, The Father moves people in and out of our lives in our seasons. People are constantly being tested; the big picture is not just about what is happening in 'our' lives. If someone cheats you, it is in his season also, the test if how you will react and how he will *teshuva*. It is when we stay stuck in the blame game and pity pot that we will not move into our next season. Rabbi Messer states that he can tell what season someone is in by the words that they speak.

We trust in The Father, The Living God to lead us into His paths of truth, righteousness, love, peace, guidance, hope, security, safeness, and mercy. "*...I trust in the mercy of God forever...*" Psalms *Tehillim* 52:8

When we are ill, we trust in The Father to heal us or guide us to the correct doctor. I trusted God when I had breast cancer to lead me unto His paths and where He wanted me to go. Information was overwhelming, I met so many doctors. Where do I go? "Trust me", was His answer.

So, we prayed, "Guide us Father – take our hand Yeshua and lead us on..." And He did – but I never took my eyes off of Him to place them on the doctors, or the nurses, or the drugs, or the homeopaths. It was Him who healed me.

My code words for trust were: steady with God.

When we lost a daughter, Tara, we trusted in God that no matter what, we loved Him and worshiped Him, as it was His Divine Plan. Was it hard? Oh, yes, and I hated it. I wanted my baby. But we had to trust.... or die such a spiritual death.

As an elderly loved one passes away, we trust in God for His greatness and the years that He gave us with that person.

Trust is all around us, yet we are misguided and put trust in people or objects, when in fact The Lord is specifically telling us to trust Him and only Him.

In the beginning of the chapter of Trust in Alan Morinis' book,[1] he quotes Rabbi Yosef Yozel Hurwitz, the Alter of Novarodok. "A person who tries to practice trust in God while leaving himself a backup plan is like a person who tries to learn how to swim but insists on keeping one foot on the ground."

This is so very true. The world we live in is so unpredictable, just the weather patterns alone are random and can be volatile. And then when we include world leaders, politicians, the friends around us, illnesses, and just plain stupidity of people, our trust can turn quickly to worry and fear.

But when we redirect our fear, to that of fear *Yirah*, (awe) of YHWH and trust in The Lord, our anxiousness will dissipate as each soul turns, *teshuva* to trust Him.

There is a difference in trusting God and being happy. God wants us to find our joy, our trust, our love, our peace, our everything in Him. That in turn gives us contentment within our soul, our very being.

The trust that He desires to be place in Him does not mean that we can rush in front of a car and trust that He will divert its path. Again, that's arrogance, stupidity and tempting The Father. Remember that The Father has bestowed upon each and everyone of us a free will, a free choice. We can choose life or death, trust or fear, worry or peace. When we put our trust in the world around us, worry and anxiousness will take over, for the world around us is full of problems, but nothing is happenstance. What a paradox!

So, as we learn to put our trust in The Father, through prayer and praise with and to Him, we lean not on our own understanding, but lean on Him. (Proverbs 3:5)

My mother was 17 when her parents took her to Europe. Her father desired, against strong advice from friends and family, to take his family into Germany. My mother recounts the story by telling us that there were German flags and swastikas, everywhere. But the streets were spookily empty. There wasn't the hustle and bustle that you might find in an ordinary situation in an ordinary busy town.

My mother's parents were allowed to only bring in enough cash for their stay; anything over would be confiscated at the border when they left Germany. The hotel they were staying at was one of the nicest, yet it too seemed abandoned.

During their visit, her mother became gravely ill. (It was the beginning of stomach cancer, which eventually claimed her life.) My grandfather could not find a doctor to help. They were stuck in Germany and their small amount of cash that they brought in was depleting fast. My mother remembers walking along the sidewalks, and being very alone. Stores were boarded up, people would not talk to her, and fear was very real.

One day, a maid of the hotel motioned for my mother to come to her, and as she did the maid slipped her the number of a doctor that might help. My grandfather was somehow able to contact that doctor who eventually came dressed very plain and quickly administered some medicine (probably morphine for pain) then left.

They bundled her up and left for the border. They were almost penniless, wondering if they would make it back into Switzerland.

As my mother told me this story, I asked her if she was ever afraid. She replied that she was and her father was very worried, too. But her mother, dying of stomach cancer, told my mother, that 17 year old child, to 'trust in The Lord'.

I asked my husband what came to his mind when I mention the word trust. His response was that trust to him means something that doesn't change. My husband is a Pastor, but first and foremost he was and is a rancher. He has trust in a cow's behavior, I have learned that. Dogs make cows nervous. But slow moving people with slow moving horses can make a cow go anywhere. His answer immediately brought me to Malachi 3:6.

"For I am YHWH I shall not change and you O sons of Ya'aqob shall not come to an end."

"Trustworthy is the Word and worthy of all acceptance. It is for this that we labor and struggle, because we trust in the Living God, who is the Savior of all men, particularly those who believe." 1Timothy 4:9, 10.

God does not change. Malachi 3:6.

1. Everyday Holiness The Path of Mussar, Alan Morinis

Notes   *Week Fourteen*   *Trust*

Code word or words:

Situations to recognize:

Trust:

Day One

Day Two

Day Three

Day Four

Day Five

Day Six

Day Seven

The Exercise:

This part of the book is different than other exercises. This requires a Concordance and a journal.

It is very important that we re- teach ourselves what trust actually is and where it is to be delegated.

There is humanly trust in this world that we cultivate, that of trust in our spouses to love us, our teachers to teach us, the police to protect us, the doctors to heal us, our children to honor us, our neighbors to like us, the firemen to save us, the politician to be forthright, the bankers to be honest, the food to be fresh, the water to be clean, the electricity on, the mechanic to fix and the baby to cry.

If one of these falters, we can always change schools, change doctors, even spouses. We can fire the policeman, the banker even impeach political parties. We can change companies, mechanics and water filters. The point here is that they could and just might cheat, steal, leave, lie or change.

But God does not and never will. Ever.

In your quest for trust, look in the concordance under trust and look up each verse. Write them down, study them, and look up the Hebrew word. Write notes in your journal.

As you work on this trait each night write down the areas that you were 'trusting' in and then when that someone or something let you down.

Why did you trust in them? And why do you feel they misused that trust?

It is important here that we do not play the blame game, 'oh you let me down, I can never trust you again.' This chapter of trust is about us finding complete trust in The Lord, no matter what or who comes our way and for what reasons.

The flip side is to awaken yourself where you might have not been a trusting person. If you have ever misused someone's trust, *teshuva*, turn - repent, ask forgiveness and go on. You may never again completely rectify the situation, but you have acknowledged it and asked forgiveness for it.

So, did you wake up this morning? Write that down! – You have trust in YHWH.

A note of encouragement: When an elderly person in our families passes on, we expect that. We say sentences like: she lived a good life…he was so old, it's better this way….etc. We don't blame God for we realize that their years have come to an end. But when we loose a child, when we have to bury one of our children, it can be easy to blame God and loose our trust in Him.

This is where we have to dig deep and totally lean on Him. He knows we are angry and wracked with grief. He knows our hurt, He feels our sorrow. Yeshua felt pain and sorrow, He wept for Miriam when Lazarus was 'asleep', and He wept over Jerusalem. Allow yourself time to grieve, allow yourself time to feel the pain. Then, begin again, with Him.

Do not build your trust on your emotions but build your trust in God by the very Word of God.

Faith

"Now faith is the substance of things hoped for, the evidence of things not seen." Hebrews 11:1

Faith is a verb. Faith is a noun. Synonyms are confidence, trust, reliance, assurance, conviction, belief, devotion, attachment and loyalty. It is a noun, for it is a thing, a substance, and yet at the same time it becomes a verb for it is the action which I move in.

We have faith in many things, some mundane some colossal. Every time I sit in a chair, I have unconscious faith that the chair will not buckle beneath me. When I fly in a plane, I have faith that the pilot knows what he is doing. I pray for safety before I fly, yet I do not pray that the chair won't break before I sit down.

And so the query of faith becomes: if the chair breaks and I land on my butt – do I loose my trust/faith in chairs – or God – or neither....but if a plane crashes....

Churches write up statements of faith. Splits are organized because of differences of faith. People are judged on their faith or lack of faith. People flock to healers with massive amounts of faith and congregants up root elders because of faith. Wars are begun on ideas of faith. People are martyred for their faith, people marry within their faith, and people change their faith.

When looking at faith through the eyes of the synonyms, I become very humanistic. I can have assurance in something, I can trust in something, in anything that I choose then again I can change that trust and change the direction of my faith. I can be loyal one day, and withdrawn the next.

My devotion will be rock solid on Tuesday and on Thursday I'm lukewarm. My faith can waver. I can actually say: "Oh, I've lost faith in him/her/them/it...."

Within the *mishnahs* of *Pirkei Avos*, there is a lesson of man abiding in God's word because he agrees. The Sages teach that that is a very dangerous place to be, for he may disagree tomorrow. We agree one day and then change our mind the next day – hence we are agreeing or disagreeing with God's principles. His very word!

We must abide in God's Torah because that is His Will, not because we disagree or agree, and that is the quintessential motivation of our faith.

So it is with faith. Our faith can and will be wavering, but YHWH's never is. We do not trust in our faith, but in His Faithfulness, [1]. Our faith can be weak, so learn to trust in His Faithfulness, subsequently our faith becomes stronger as we become in the likeness of Him.

When I was going through cancer treatment, there were a few religious people, people stuck in a religious system, and not abiding in His Kingdom, that had the idea that I didn't have 'enough' faith for I wasn't healed without surgery or chemo. After all, if I had 'enough' faith I would be healed!

Well, I was healed. It was through The Father that He led me to the places of treatment. I had faith in His Wisdom, not my own. I had faith in His powers, not my own. I had, I have faith in His faithfulness, not my own.

In the *Tanakh*, the word 'faith' is used twice. (Strongs Concordance) Deuteronomy 32:20 where it is translated as *emuwn* pronounced ay-moon, meaning trustworthiness, and it is coming from the root word *aman*, pronounced aw-man; with meanings of: to support, to trust, to parent, to nurse, to believe, to be permanent, to be sure, to turn to the right.

In Habakkuk 2:4 it is the Hebrew word *emunah* meaning security, stability, steady, steadfastness, faith, truly, truth, verily.

There are two full columns in the concordance with verses in the New Testament from the Greek word, *pisteuo* pronounced pist-yoo. Also, *pistis* pronounced pis-tis. It means to have faith upon, to respect, to entrust, and to commit to put trust with. It comes from the root word *peitho*. It's meaning: to assent, to rely, agree, assure, believe, have confidence in, be wax, confident, make friend, obey, persuade, trust and yield.

Faithful, faithfully and faithfulness in the Tanakh is the word *emunah*. That word is translated as steady or steadfast. When you connect steady or steadfast with The Father, *Elohim*, then the two become one. A human can lose their steadfastness, their steadiness within the boundaries of their lives. That is why it is so important that we connect with The Fathers' faithfulness. In that way, we connect with the source. We have to learn to have faith in Him and not because of our beliefs, for beliefs will and do differ and change and grow and dissipate.

Again, there are seven covenants of YHWH. Each one is stacked upon the prior like a pancake; they are the foundation for the other.

1. The Covenant of Eden
2. The Covenant of Adam
3. The Covenant of Noah
4. The Covenant of Abraham
5. The Covenant of Moses
6. The Covenant of David
7. The Renewed Covenant

The Abrahamic Covenant is of faith. By faith in God, Abraham left his father. By faith in God, he went to a different land. By faith in God his wife of aged years had a son and by faith in God he took that son to the mountain. *"And Abraham said, My son, God will provide Himself a lamb for a burnt offering: so they went both of them together."* Genesis *Bereshith* 22:8

Hebrews 11 is often called the faith chapter. It is the very substance that we survive on. I often wondered, for those that do not believe in any God, and they are just here until they die, then why even bother? What's the point of life? But it is by faith that our hope is built on. It is faith that keeps us going. Our faith in Him.

We are also cautioned that faith without works is dead, James 2:17. So the two, faith and works, connect like a thread. What are the works that connect us to the faith of the Father? The works are of the Father. His will be done on Earth as it is in Heaven. What is The Lords will that we do? To have the faith in The Father that comes from The Father only by The Father, Elohim, Adonai. By doing His Will it will bring us into that covering. We acknowledge His Will, His Sabbath, His Appointed Times, His Commandments, and His Mercy, His *Chesed*, His Salvation.

Or, we can make up our own chess game: if I do this, then I will have that. Or if I say this, he will say that and then I can do this and that and on and on we play. Or, we can submit to the Will of The Father and cleave to His Faithfulness, knowing that we are His and He walks before us.

"Know therefore that YHWH, Elohim He is Adonai, the faithful Adonai, which keeps covenant and mercy with them that love Him and keep His Commandments to a thousand generations." Deuteronomy *Devarim* 7:9

"Thy mercy O LORD is in the heavens and thy faithfulness reaches into the clouds." Psalms *Tehillim* 36:5

If we abide in our own faith, we will run into trouble. If we abide in His faithfulness, it is a promise that He will keep us from evil. *"But YHWH is faithful who will establish you and keep you from evil."* 2Thessalonians 3:3

God will establish me! I am not my own, so if I walk in the camp, God will establish me and keep me from evil....if I stray from the camp, I can be walking in evil. How can I establish myself? I did not create myself — therefore, how could I possible create my own faith.

Alan Morinis teaches that the door, or gate, to faith is not opened by rational thought.[2] If anything, rational thought will keep us from growing in faith, for we can only grow in faith when we seek His will and His Faithfulness. 'I have faith in Him'. I don't have faith in me.

A PET Scan is a way to tell if cancer cells are still lurking in your body either after surgery or after chemo. It is similar to a MRI, as you enter a cylinder and slide in and out for about 45 minutes. There is nothing more nerve wracking than going through this test, listening to the hum and the clanging, wondering: Is it gone?

Cancer is a disease, a killer that lurks behind the darkness of our minds. It is always there. Every little cough, every ache, cancer patients wonder: is it back? It's not like high blood pressure that can be managed with a pill. Cancer is unlike a broken arm that can be fixed. Cancer is there, prowling around, with no mercy for race, gender or financial standing.

It is very easy for panic to set in. Okay, this is it, I'm going to die. First I have to go through surgery, chemo and radiation and then I'll die. Those are very real thoughts we all face, from very rational people, some who believe in God and those who do not. After cancer stricken people search on the internet, we are even more confused. What do I do? Who do I trust? Where do I go?

Those that walk with God, we stop and we pray. We realize that we can not do this by ourselves, we ask for guidance and direction. That is the very first step towards complete faith. In Him. And faith carries a person's soul.[3]

In anything you do, be it very grand or miniscule, the very first step is to stop and pray. That is faith, knowing that we can not do this alone. That is the faith that He requires of us, whether the answers are what we desire or not, whether the outcome is what we demand or not, the faith that He requires is not optional or debatable. It is a surrendering faith, a complete acknowledgement that we are His and He is THE LORD.

Yeshua came to this world to show us that exact and complete faith. None of us know the outcome of our lives, but He knew His. And still He walked in complete obedience to the Father and His will, constantly glorifying The Father and telling His people that He does nothing on His own, but the will of The Father who sent Him.

"I will sing of the mercies of YHWH forever: with my mouth will I make known His faithfulness to all generations." Psalms *Tehillim* 89:1, 105:8

"YHWH is faithful, by whom you were called to the fellowship of His Son Yeshua our LORD." 1Corinthians 1:9

1. Rabbi Messer, Simchat Torah Beit Midrash, Denver CO
2. Alan Morinis, Everyday Holiness The Path of Mussar
3. Pastor Jay Howard, Simchat haMashiach Beit Emunah

This part of the exercises is somewhat different than the previous chapters. One can wake up in the morning and say: today I will keep my patience when my child spills the milk.

But faith is a process and to grow in faith is a one on one life learning experience with God. It is by prayer, fasting, trust, love, obedience, and surrendering our will completely. It is walking with humility with The Father. It is acceptance of the seasons that He places in front of us. It is surrender to His will – completely. Faith can not be taught.

We can encourage one another in faith; we can even wrongly hurt one another for lack of faith. But we can not teach faith.

So, for this part, find the code word that reminds you of faith and one that will also trigger your brain to stop and pray and ask for faith. *Emunah*

Look for situations that may arise. For the weekly writing, there are Scripture verses to look up. Remember that you will grow in faith as you seek The Father and His will. Do not be discouraged. Don't look for ways to counter attack your faith and learn to recognize people that want to lessen you faith. Stay away from negative forces. Surround yourself with His word and people that will encourage you. And, encourage others. Pray with people, pray for people. Bless YHWH.

Change Your Life

<u>Notes</u>　　　　<u>Week Fifteen</u>　　　<u>Faith</u>

Code word or words:

Situations to recognize:

Faith:

Day One:	Hebrews 11:3	Genesis 9:16-17
Day Two:	Mathew 17:20	2Timothy 2:13-19
Day Three:	Mark 11:22-24	Deuteronomy 7:8,9
Day Four:	Romans 1:17	Psalms 121:3-8
Day Five:	1Peter 1:7-9	2Peter 3:9
Day Six:	1John 5:3-5	Genesis 28:15
Day Seven:	James 1:6	Isaiah 54:9, 10

Change Your Life

At 9:22 this morning, Sunday as I was working on the 'Faith' Chapter, our son called. He was on shift with the fire department, so I sensed something was wrong, as he never calls while working. The sound of his voice confirmed that suspicion.

"Max, are you okay?" I responded.

"No, Mom, I'm not." He answered.

Any parent will validate that those are dreaded words that will rock us to the core, and test our inner strengths. Our faith will waver, even briefly but it will waver so we reach down into our souls and cling to God. Praying, asking, and seeking.

It is amazing to me how God brings us full circle into the realm where we personally need work, guidance, help, testing, whatever you desire to call it, it is Him shaping us. It is very painful and uncomfortable to be that jar of clay, that iron which is sharpened by iron, that gold that passes through the refiner's fire.

The department received a call for a drunken person that had hit his head, or was wounded. My son was the lead medical person and so it was his call. Both EMT's and crew were trying to help this person, who was very combative towards the medical crew. He had to be restrained and then he proceeded to spit in my sons face. They transported him, where at the hospital he not only received care for his wounds, but had blood drawn to see if he was carrying HIV, AIDS or Hepatitis. Max also had blood drawn to give the doctors a base if the results on the injured/combative person come back positive. Then, Max will again have blood drawn in four weeks to see if he has contracted any disease.

Trust, faith, anxiety, nervousness, worry, trust, faith, anxiety, nervousness and on and on we go.

Immediately, I sent out emails requesting prayer. The first reply I received was from a lady at Simchat Torah Beit Midrash.

"If you diligently heed the voice of the LORD, your God and do what is right in His sight, give ear to His commandments and keep all of His statutes, I will put none of the diseases on you which I have brought on the Egyptians. For I am the LORD Who heals you." Exodus *Shemoth* 15:26

That is the essence of faith; works, obedience, trust, mercy, love and grace.

It is the faith we have in Him in the things unseen.

Faith is not an emotion – yet rather an objective trust placed in a very real God –
Bruce Bickel

Forgiveness

Calach

Calach, callach and *c'liych* are the Hebrew words used for forgiveness. The other English translations are spare, pardon and ready to forgive. Another Hebrew word is *nasa'* which translates: spare, forgive, lift up, respect, set up, carry, and ease, exact, rise up and magnify.

The Greek word used in the NT is *aphiemi'* to forgive, forsake, lay aside, to leave, yield up and remit. Some English synonyms of forgiveness are: pardon, clemency, pity, mercy, absolution, amnesty, exoneration, and exculpation. It was interesting that the antonym was 'blame'.

Just tonight, as I was working on this chapter, my husband was commenting on the English language. The Scriptures because of the language crossing over from Hebrew to Greek to English lose so much depth.

Forgiveness. What do you think? Do you think: I forgive so and so. But look at the rich meanings in the Hebrew: to lay aside, to exalt, to lift up. When I look at those meanings, and put them together, I get a better understanding. To lay aside. To exalt. To lift up, to pardon.

If I live in unforgiveness, can I really lay aside anything? Can I truly exalt that person? It is when I seek forgiveness, through the help of the Holy Spirit, and then I can uplift that person that has wronged me.

We are commanded to forgive others, Colossians 3:12, 13. We are told to be kind hearted and forgiving, Ephesians 4:32. We are told that if we forgive then we are forgiven, Matthew 6:14. We are told to confess our sins and that He is faithful to forgive us, 1John 1:9.

We are promised that The Father forgives all our iniquities and heals our disease. Psalms 103:3. He is the great forgiver and healer.

So, forgiveness goes beyond the mere lip service of simply saying to another person, I forgive you. And in the influence of the Jezebel spirit, one would say: "I'm sorry you were hurt." But that is neither true repentance nor asking of forgiveness. It is forgiveness in the disguise of a judgment. (If you weren't hurt this wouldn't have happened....)

When we put the above true meanings of forgiveness into the word, really attach them to the word forgiveness, then one can grasp the deepness of the mercy that God has upon us. I think of all the things I have done or said and the ways that I have acted. Some of them quite horribly, actually, especially to my parents when I was a young wild youth. So God, in His infinite wisdom, grace and mercy not only forgives us, He then pardons us and lifts us up.

Now, that I know of the depths of His forgiveness, I can retrace my actions and remember when I have come before YHWH with a repentant heart and have asked of His great forgiveness. I have felt an exuberance to 'try again'. Wasn't that His laying of His pardon upon me? Wasn't that His lifting me up to give me the courage to forgive others, myself, and go again? He was exalting me to keep going.

So, purposefully, this is the last character trait of the book. Yet it is the most important. It's like the fortune cookie at the Chinese Restaurant. The food is wonderful, but we all wait to crack open the semi-stale cookie to read that fortune!

One can go through the emotions of all the other character traits. We can develop patience, and can learn to honor people. We can learn to be generous, and acquire silence at the right times. But, if we harbor bitterroot judgment in our lives, if we have any amount of unforgiveness – we die spiritually and our character traits, be they good or bad, will have the smell of unforgiveness. There will be a stench.

Rabbi Messer [1], quotes Rabbi Ted Falson:

"Jewish tradition identifies three stages in the process of forgiveness, whether you are being forgiven or you are forgiving others. The steps are identified by the words: *s'lichach* – forgiveness; *m'chilach* – letting go, and *kapporah* - atonement. Forgiveness begins with the conscious intention to forgive. But if the process ends there, the feelings of guilt or resentment reappear when you least expect them. Letting go means: I no longer need the past to have been any different than it was. At this stage you may remember the pain but you are no longer consumed either with guilt or resentment. With atonement, you can accomplish something positive that otherwise wouldn't have been possible. You still remember and you still may feel the pain but the act of atonement transforms the pain into a blessing."

A great barrier that can and will keep God's blessings out of our lives is unforgivenes and bitter root in our hearts toward others and us. The very core of unforgiveness and bitter root will then become the idol of our heart as we keep playing the victim.

Change Your Life

By holding onto that anger and unforgiveness we then become the center of the story. Anger, if allowed to build into unforgiveness, is a way for a person to keep themselves the center of *their* story. Anger therefore can become addictive and it turns into unforgiveness, which then becomes the idol of our heart. Our hurt remains where love should grow.

How can we honestly pray for a person when we harbor unforgiveness? How can we pray for anyone? Isn't that exactly what Yeshua meant when He commanded us to lay our gifts (literally ourselves) at the altar and seek the person that we have offended or that we have an offense with? How can we work on our character traits when unforgiveness rules our hearts?

Approximately twenty minutes before my double mastectomy surgery, Mrs. Messer and my husband were in the tiny prep room with me, keeping me in light spirits. They had prayed with me, and we all had a sense of peace about the surgery and surgeons. All the tubes were hooked up, needles in place in my veins, the right drips going, all was set. We were just waiting for the nurse to come and administer a drug to knock me out before they wheeled me away.

Suddenly, Mrs. Messer turned to me and said, "Who haven't you forgiven in your life?"

I must have look perplexed for she asked it again.

I thought about her question, what is she talking about? I've been a Christian for umpteen years. Now I walk in Torah; hey, I have forgiven everyone!

She asked it a third time, and looked deep into my eyes. Her gaze was piercing.

It was at that moment that The Lord revealed to me I still harbored unforgiveness towards someone and when I briefly thought about that person, I became agitated again! Wow! What an eye opener!

We prayed together and I released that anger and forgave them. It was a huge burden lifted off of me, one that I didn't even know I was carrying around.

Seconds, literally seconds later, the nurse walked in, said 'good night' and I was out.

A lot of illnesses are linked to bitterroot judgment. A lot of problems, anger issues, divorces, kids running away, suicides, addictions with substances and murder have deep roots to unforgiveness.

Is that the walk that our King of Kings has for us? Does He desire that we remain in the mud and muck of unforgiveness? Or is He in our lives to set us free. Doesn't the truth truly set us free?

In a confrontation with my spouse, I have learned to break out of the argument by walking out of the room and pray for him and myself. I pray to stop the craziness. However, when I have been hurt by his words, I have desired to repeat those hurtful words to him. I wanted to come back into the room, with forgiveness, yet with a chip on my shoulder and let him know just how much he did hurt me. But I forgave him! Really? Or was I harboring my hurt.

Forgiveness is an act of self. I can and should forgive someone even if they have not asked for it. What if I was wronged by a person who is now dead? Or in prison? I can't harbor unforgivenness. I must release that spirit of bitterroot. My bitterroot will not affect the dead person or a person in prison, or even my next door neighbor. But, it will affect me. I have to completely let go and give it to Yeshua. Acknowledge – resist- reverse it.

If someone asks of my forgiveness, I must not hesitate and roll it over and over in my mind repeating the pain and telling myself, "Yeah, you DID hurt me!" or "I'm not ready yet."

No, I must forgive on the spot, to release them of their burden as I am released of mine by the grace of The Father.

If I have wronged a person, quickly I should ask forgiveness from them. It will destroy our very souls if we have hurt someone and not ask of their forgiveness. In addition to that, aren't we still hurting the other person by holding onto our pride and not seeking reconciliation? You don't have to become bosom buddies, just apologize for a wrong committed.

Forgiveness isn't easy, especially in forgiving ourselves. In the Scriptures, Yeshua tells us that we will do greater works. What possibly could that greater works be? – He was God incarnate!

Rabbi Messer [2], taught on that some years back. Yeshua never had to forgive Himself, for He was perfect. Could it be the greater works are forgiving ourselves and others?

We harbor so much guilt that we can literally kill ourselves, whether slowly by illnesses or addictions or quickly by suicide. However, in a diminutive way, guilt can be an excellent emotion *if* we recognize it quickly: what is Yeshua trying to tell me here? "I feel so guilty…." Then I ask myself: "why do I feel guilty?" Well, maybe I need to apologize to someone – quickly. The Holy Spirit is working within me at that very moment. Release that person, release myself and release the bondage of guilt.

But, if I harbor that guilt and let it build with in me, then two things are possible. First, I become the center of my story, for it is I that feels guilty. I can't crawl out of my hole, I am consumed with my guilt, and I am not in obedience with The Father to ask for forgiveness. I am allowing the enemy to work in my life and destroy me as well as the others that I have hurt. I die in guilt. I, I, I, I….. Suddenly, the whole wrong that I may have committed is centered on me, myself and I. I am filled with self-debasement, which will never, ever bring glory to The Father.

Secondly, those that I have hurt can also become filled with guilt if they are not spiritually strong or wise in their walk with The Lord. It is very possible that they will harbor unforgiveness towards me, and then they become ridden with guilt because they never forgave me. It can be a very disastrous stumbling block and a vicious cycle.

A woman has come into a situation involving her new husband and his two teenage sons. She has behaved quite poorly, harboring anger, bad mouthing the biological mother, and yelling at the father, her husband. Subsequently, the two boys will have nothing to do with her, and their father since she is constantly with him.

When one of the boys was asked how things are going, and how is your Dad; his response was souring.

"Things are going pretty good. She's almost ready to apologize to me, but not Henry, yet." (the younger boy)

Not ready to apologize? Isn't that arrogance to the core? And what if something tragic happens – and the opportunity to apologize is lost.

This cycle has continued. The woman has left, and now the man, left alone to clean up the whirlwind has repeated those exact words: "I'm not ready to forgive so and so yet."

The right to hold onto our hurt and unforgiveness is a man made act, it is nothing granted from The Father.

Yet forgiveness is not just forgetting, or excusing or denying behavior or numbing ourselves to pain. We just can't forget on command and 'get over it!' I am not a robot and neither are you.

Forgiveness isn't forgetting, for if we forget the past, we repeat it. My daughter gave her phone number out to someone she shouldn't have. He eventually asked for forgiveness, but she does not forget the consequences and is a lot wiser to whom she gives her number out.

Neither is forgiveness excusing our own behavior or someone else's. We are always given a choice in how we are going to act. The past tells us where we were and what we did but does not lock us into staying there repeating that behavior. [3]

Forgiveness really isn't acceptance, either. We shouldn't accept the pain inflicted upon us by others, or accept the pain that we inflict on others. That would develop into a much calloused person. Acceptance would mean that forgiveness is not necessary. So, acceptance as surrender is not forgiveness. [4]

Forgiveness isn't denial, either. If I have done something horrible to someone, denial doesn't and never will rectify the situation. I must accept reality as reality and own up to the concrete fact that I have done something horrible and ask forgiveness. The same is true if something horrible is done to me. If I deny that reality, then I push it deep within me, and it will fester there, like a cancer. I must accept the reality that something horrible happened and forgive even if the perpetrator never asks for forgiveness. Our supreme example in this case is our Messiah as He asks The Father *to forgive them for they know not what they do.*

Neither is numbness forgiveness. There are some people that pretend to feel no pain. They claim that they have become so spiritual that they feel no pain. And when they hurt someone else, they respond to that person's pain by blaming them accordingly, as in not being spiritual enough.

Our Messiah was not numb to others pain. King David was not numb to the pain he inflicted by causing the death of one of his soldiers. Emotions are given to us by The Father Almighty that we may experience His reality and truly feel for one another.

Forgiveness is not denial, acceptance, forgetting or numbness. Forgiveness is letting go. [5] To let go means that I no longer need to live in the narrow mind of clinging to my hurt and memories. I go forward with the Messiah. Keep moving forward!

As we humble ourselves before The Father to let go of the pain and hurt and seek forgiveness and truly forgive others, our character traits will smooth out. What needs to be more will be more. What needs to be less will be less. Forgiveness is the key that binds all of us together - His children.

Everyday, seek out the verses about forgiveness. I could list them all in this book, but the impact would not be the same as when you have to look them up for yourselves and grasp the entire context.

Everyday pray about forgiveness. Who do I need to forgive? Who do I need to ask forgiveness of?

Be astute in catching yourself in bringing up the pain, and remembering the hurt. Why are you bringing it up again? I need to ask myself, what am

I trying to accomplish by reliving it? Is this really how I want to glorify The Father?

So, we get on our face, we fast, we pray, we ask forgiveness. We forgive those around us and we forgive ourselves.

We are here to build the Kingdom of Yeshua. How can we do that when we are not in harmony with our brothers? This is a huge challenge for each of us.

Being in harmony just doesn't create a nice atmosphere, it creates synergy. Synergy can be explained as losing a toe, it will totally affect my balance, but I can manage. However, if I lose all my toes, the balance will be gone and I will have to relearn to walk. Just a little toe makes so much difference! That's synergy!

This is the kind of synergy spoken of in Deuteronomy *Devarim* 32:30 when it speaks of one chasing a thousand and the two putting ten thousand to flight. Our minds rationalized that if one chases a thousand, we think of two chasing two thousand. But God reminds us of His unity within us and we are ten times more powerful when we join together. One to one yet two to ten!

Forgiveness is the link.

Rabbi Sha'ul, or Paul admonishes us to have loving kindness and charity and love. Without these our acts of *mitzvoh* are nothing. What better way to show loving kindness than to forgive someone or to ask for forgiveness.

Rabbi Shapiro teaches that forgiveness and loving-kindness are inextricably connected to each other. He goes on to say that loving-kindness that is not grounded in forgiveness is not true loving-kindness. Forgiveness not grounded in loving-kindness is not true forgiveness. What a great parallel.

Years ago, my mother shared this poem with me:

Drop a stone into the water
In a moment it is gone
But there are hundreds of ripples
Circling on and on
Say an unkind word
This moment
And in a moment it is gone
But there are hundreds of ripples
Circling on and on
Say a word of cheer and splendor

*In a moment it is gone
But there are hundreds of ripples
Circling on and on*

Dear Heavenly Father, I come before you with a repentant heart and ask forgiveness. I also forgive those that have hurt me and I let go of the pain and I ask that you help me in not clinging to the memories, but push me forward. I desire to walk as Yeshua walked, in lovingkindness and forgiveness. Please guide me, direct my path and help me to truly forgive. In Yeshua's Name I ask these things, Amen and Amen..

1. Rabbi Ralph Messer, Simchat Torah Beit Midrash, Denver CO
2. Rabbi Ralph Messer, Simchat Torah Beit Midrash, Denver CO
3. Rabbi Rami Shapiro, The Sacred Art of Lovingkindness
4. Rabbi Rami Shapiro, The Sacred Art of Lovingkindness
5. Rabbi Rami Shapiro, The Sacred Art of Lovingkindness

Notes *Week Sixteen* *Forgiveness*

Code words: Letting go

Situations to recognize:

Forgiveness:

Day One:

Day Two:

Day Three:

Day Four:

Day Five:

Day Six:

Day Seven:

You can wash your hands but not your conscience. Forgive quickly and live.

Keep Moving Forward

We are all given free choice in this world. How we behave, how we react, what we do to ourselves and one another. We have our genetics, our DNA, our generational curses and problems. We have our good character traits and our not so good character traits. It is all in what we choose to do.

I can walk in forgiveness, or I can walk in anger. I can love or I can be bitter. I can acknowledge that anger runs in my family and deal with it, or I can deny what the Scriptures say and simply succumb to the fact that I am angry.

My thirteen year old son is studying the book of Joshua. One of the questions on the test was: What did God command to be Israel's first act of preparation for the battles ahead? The answer: circumcision of the males.

God is telling His people that they cannot go into battle until they are circumcised. Today it is a circumcision of the heart, which is the same process.

Physical circumcision if done correctly at 8 days old is quickly forgotten for as soon as the baby starts nursing, he forgets the physical pain. I think it's harder on the parents. A physical thing can be easy. But to circumcise my heart? What does that mean? It means to cut. My heart does not belong to me, but it belongs to God.

Only if we circumcise ourselves can we go into the battle to win. And God constantly tells us that the battle is His. If we do not obey His commands; we will not win the battle, we will stay stuck in that place in the wilderness. We will not move from one season to another, we will not learn from the test. But as soon as we obey – listen – *Shema!* to His voice and circumcise our hearts, we can enter into battle and win because of Him, and for Him and not because of anything we might do. The glory will go to The Father and not of our own doing.

Pastor Jay Howard teaches that we will descend to cross over and we will ascend to be victorious, as in crossing the Red Sea, the descent came before the ascent onto dry land where the Israelites were victorious. There will be a descent before the ascent, (Rabbi Messer).

In the book of Joshua when they crossed the Jordan River, which in Hebrew *Yarden* actually means 'to descend' it was their descent and their victory came after the ascent to, the cross over into Jericho, which they conquered. When we cross, *awbar,* cross-over it is a covenant act. One of the definitions of *awbar is* to pass through the parts of covenant. As in the book of Joshua they descended down to the Jordan to cross through it, to pass between the parts, which are likened to the crossing of the Red Sea. It is the covenant made by YHWH as He crossed through the animal parts with Abraham in Genesis 15.

It shouts of faith, of lovingkindness, of joy, of trust, of truth and honor. It is our covenant act. When we react to God's Torah, we are then elevated into our ascent. And it is all for the glory to YHWH. Can I glorify myself just because I am in obedience to His Word? Or, will The Father receive the glory.

I want to thank you for purchasing this book. My desire is that we all glorify The Father in our lives. My desire is that we do not waste another day living in fear, anger, bitterroot judgment or sadness.

Life is too short, and the days that are gone we never get back. We will never get this moment back. We must live each day to its fullest and protect our boundaries that YHWH has established with love and kindness.

To waste another precious day in the wounded life of self centeredness only wastes the time that we could be spending showing the light, the salt, the love of our Lord, *Yeshua HaMashiach*. I encourage you – go forward.

But please, don't beat yourself up either, if you don't change right away. It's a process, it's a lifetime process. But there is always the start.

This was a hard winter on us. One night as my husband and I tried to sleep our bedroom filled with smoke from the woodstove. Suddenly a noise, resembling thunder filled our room. It was solid frozen snow/ice that fell from the roof ridge to the bedroom roof. It came sliding off and took our stove pipe with it. We sat up in bed just in time to see the pipe sailing across the white snow and land straight up, stuck. (The moon was very bright that night) I felt like I was on the Titanic.

The work that now lay ahead of my husband was going to be hard. Getting on a slippery roof, shoveling 2 feet of snow/ice and then fixing a stovepipe, was not going to be easy, especially at age 50something. Neither of us was looking forward to it. We complained and longed for a warm sunny beach to lay on with a cold glass of ice tea.

At the moment, it was where we were at. And I am quite sure that God understood. He didn't rebuke us for not being perfect, for not thanking Him at that instant for the huge amounts of snow we had received through out the winter, and for the work that lay ahead of us. (Actually, I didn't do a thing; my husband had to fix it all. I just watched him on the slippery roof and prayed for his safety).

I love God, as you do. I love life, as you do. I love my family and friends, as you do. Breathe, listen, and be still. You're gonna make it.

Yehudah ben Tema says to be bold as a leopard, light as an eagle, swift as a deer and strong as a lion in order to carry out the will of your Father in Heaven. This sentence gives us a fourfold visual of our lives with The Father; the leopard, courageous and brave and the eagle, soaring above all and radiating brilliance. We are to be as swift as the deer, quick and leaping above trouble, and to be strong as a lion. To be like The lion of the Tribe of Judah.

In working on these traits, remember those four attributes. And as you correct the traits in your life that you want to change, be the leopard, the eagle, the deer and the lion. Always remember that The will of our Father is to glorify Him and walk with Yeshua. You can do this – keep your focus and keep moving forward! But in all things, remember that we are the enemy of ourselves, and we can overcome that enemy. But to be successful in that we must recognize, repent, renounce, resist and reverse. Always reverse the negative with a positive, always replace worry with joy, fear with truth, dis-honor with honor, and criticalness with lovingkindness.

In the book of Revelation we are referred to as overcomers, that we need to be overcomers and that we must conquer as overcomers. Do not despair, and do not belittle yourself. Do breathe.

I am not a counselor; I can only offer this book to help put you on the right track. If you are hurting or wounded or seriously depressed, please seek help from your Rabbi or Pastor or counselor. Also know that God will never leave you nor forsake you, that is His complete truth and promise.

I know it's hard, life is hard. Let's make it better. Blessings to you all,

Vickie Howard

CPSIA information can be obtained
at www.ICGtesting.com
Printed in the USA
BVOW08s0714070417
480627BV00001B/3/P